Self-assessment for business excellence

WITHDRAWN

QUALITY
— IN —
ACTION

●

SERIES EDITOR
BARRIE DALE
UMIST

Self-assessment for business excellence

David Lascelles and Roy Peacock

McGRAW-HILL BOOK COMPANY

London · New York · St Louis · San Francisco · Auckland
Bogotá · Caracas · Lisbon · Madrid · Mexico · Milan
Montreal · New Delhi · Panama · Paris · San Juan
São Paulo · Singapore · Sydney · Tokyo · Toronto

Published by McGraw-Hill Book Company Europe
Shoppenhangers Road, Maidenhead, Berkshire SL6 2QL, England
Telephone 01628 23432
Fax 01628 770224

British Library Cataloguing in Publication Data
Lascelles, D.M.
  Self-assessment for Business Excellence.
  – (Quality in Action Series)
  I. Title II. Peacock, Roy III. Series
  658.562

  ISBN 0-07-709186-8

Library of Congress Cataloging-in-Publication Data

A catalogue record for this book is available from
the Library of Congress.

McGraw-Hill

A Division of The **McGraw·Hill** Companies

1234 BL 99876

Typeset by BookEns Ltd, Royston, Herts.
and printed and bound by Biddles Ltd, Guildford and King's Lynn

Printed on permanent paper in compliance with ISO Standard 9706

Contents

Series Preface

Quality is regarded by most producers, customers and consumers as more important than ever before in their manufacturing, service and purchasing strategies. If you doubt this just think of the unsatisfactory examples of quality you have personally experienced, the bad feelings it gave you, the resulting actions you took and the people you told about the experience and outcomes. The concept of Total Quality Management (TQM) is increasingly being adopted by organizations as the means of satisfying the needs and expectations of their customers.

TQM has been practised by the major Japanese manufacturing companies for the last 30 or so years. Their commitment to continuous and company-wide quality improvement has provided them with the foundation to capture markets the world over. In response to this competitive pressure Western manufacturing companies, first in the United States and then in Europe, started to embrace the TQM ethic. They were followed by commercial and service type organizations. The superior performing Western organizations have now some 15 years or so of TQM operating experience. These organizations have now integrated the principles and practices of TQM into the way they run their business. This is one indicator of the effectiveness of TQM. Senior management are judged on results and if TQM did not improve business performance, they would simply rechannel the resources in other directions.

TQM is a subject and management philosophy in which there appears to be an unquenchable thirst for knowledge, despite the considerable volume of published material. In recent times the interest in TQM has been fuelled by the Malcolm Baldrige National Quality Award and the European Quality Award. These awards, based on a model of TQM, are being increasingly used by organizations as part of their business improvement process. This interest in the subject has continued in spite of some surveys and reports indicating that TQM is not working. There is also evidence that the concept is being regurgitated under a number of other guises. The objective of this major 'Quality in Action' book series is to help satisfy this need and fill what we believe are gaps in the existing range of current books. It is also obvious from the arguments advanced from some quarters that there is still a lack of understanding of TQM and what it is about. Hopefully the books in the series will help to improve the level of understanding.

McGraw-Hill has already published books by three of the best known and internationally respected quality management experts – Crosby, Feigenbaum and Juran. The 'Quality in Action' series will build upon the work of these three men; this in itself will be a challenge.

I was honoured when asked by McGraw-Hill to be the 'Quality in Action' book series editor. I have been involved in industrially-based TQM research for the last 14 or so years and from this experience believe I am well placed to identify the aspects of TQM that need to be addressed by new books on the subject.

The prime focus of the series is management and the texts have been prepared from this standpoint. However, undergraduate and postgraduate students will also find the books of considerable benefit in understanding the concept, principles, elements and practices of TQM, the associated quality management systems, tools and techniques, the means of introducing, developing and sustaining TQM and the associated difficulties, and how to integrate TQM into the business practices of an organization.

One objective of the series is to provide some general TQM reading as guidance for management in introducing, developing and sustaining a process of continuous and company-wide quality improvement. It focuses on manufacturing, commercial and service situations. We are looking for recognized writers (academics, consultants and practitioners) who can address the subject from a European perspective. The books appearing on this theme do not duplicate already published material, rather they build upon, enhance and develop the TQM wisdom and address the subject from a new perspective. A second objective is to provide texts on aspects of TQM not adequately covered by current books. For example, TQM and human resources, sustaining TQM, TQM: corporate culture and organizational change, partnership sourcing and supply chain management, TQM and business strategy. It is likely that the authors of these books will be from disciplines (e.g., accounting, economic, psychology, human resources) not traditionally associated with quality management. A third objective is to provide texts which deal with quality management systems, tools and techniques in a practical 'how-to' manner.

The first four books in the series: *Japanese-led companies: Understanding how to make them your customers*; *Quality of service: Making it really work*; *Motivating your organization: Achieving business success through reward and recognition*, and *Communicating change* have been well received by the business community and are helping to address these objectives.

My commitment to this series is such that I am prepared to allocate time from my considerable research, teaching and advisory activities in order to ensure that it meets and hopefully exceeds the needs and expectations of our readers.

B.G. Dale, Series Editor

About the Series Editor

Dr Barrie Dale is Reader in Quality Management at the Manchester School of Management, UMIST and Director of the UMIST Quality Management Centre. The Centre is involved in three major activities: research into TQM; the Centre houses the Ford Motor Company's Northern Regional Centre for training suppliers in Statistical Process Control; and the operation of a TQM Multi-Company Teaching Programme involving collaborators from a variety of industrial and business environments. Dr Dale also co-ordinates the Bowater Corrugated Division Multi-Institute Teaching Programme. He is a non-executive director of Manchester Circuits Ltd, a company specializing in the manufacture of high technology and complex printed circuit boards.

Dr Dale is co-editor of the International Journal of Quality and Reliability Management, now in its twelfth volume. He is also co-author of *Managing Quality, Quality Costing, Quality Improvement Through Standards, Total Quality and Human Resources: An Executive Guide* and *The Road to Quality* and has published over 220 papers on the subject of quality management. Dr Dale has led four missions to Japan of European executives to study the application of TQM in major Japanese manufacturing organizations. He is the international quality management advisor to the South African Quality Institute. Dr Dale has also been closely associated with the Hong Kong Government Industry Department in preparing a series of booklets on quality management for their 'Make it Better in Hong Kong' campaign.

Preface

Business success today is judged mainly on financial performance. To achieve business success through good financial performance company executives tend to introduce a never-ending series of initiatives to improve results. However, these initiatives are often introduced without any clear overall plan. Sometimes initiatives in one area or function are seemingly in conflict with other initiatives introduced elsewhere in the organization. There is seldom any overall management or coordination of these initiatives nor any clear idea of how they will influence financial performance.

While all companies strive for business success, world-class companies aim for excellence and recognition. Business excellence links the principles of Total Quality Management (TQM) to a wider perspective of the company's stakeholders and their needs. This is a perspective that focuses on what will satisfy and create value for all the company's principal stakeholders: its customers, its shareholders, its employees and society. It is a holistic approach to managing a business that is starting to become the norm for leading companies worldwide.

How can organizations achieve business excellence? The European Business Excellence Model provides a vehicle for achieving business excellence. It provides an integrated structure for coordinating and managing all improvement initiatives to create outstanding business performance. The European Business Excellence Model, which was developed by the European Foundation for Quality Management (EFQM) and which underpins the European, the UK and some other national quality awards, is a flowchart of how an excellent company operates. Increasingly, many companies seeking business excellence are assessing themselves against the nine criteria of the model first to understand fully their position today and then to use this benchmark to pursue continuous improvement. The model enables the executive management team to view the overall business as a network of interrelated value creation processes and to carry out self-assessment to identify the organization's strengths and areas for improvement.

Unlike traditional methods of assessing business success which focus solely on the financial results, in business excellence self-assessment equal emphasis is given to 'cause' (enablers) and 'effect' (results). It helps managers to answer that nagging question: 'Are we taking the right actions to produce the right results?'

Excellent companies do two things: they focus on creating value for their principal stakeholders and they make the right decisions to create value. The characteristics of business excellence are explored in Chapter 1 from the viewpoint of what will constitute business success in the future and how companies can learn from this. One thing is certain, the achievement of business excellence will require companies to become learning organizations: to learn about themselves and about their stakeholders' needs. Business excellence self-assessment provides the keys to learning.

The European Business Excellence Model is itself a framework for learning, providing a set of benchmarks against which any organization can measure its achievements and map future progress. The model represents how an excellent company will look some five or so years into the future rather than common best practice today. Chapter 2 describes the structure of the model, highlights its constituent parts and outlines the assessment scoring system.

There are several ways in which self-assessment can be carried out. These range from simple questionnaires through management workshops to the simulation of a full European Quality Award application. Various factors will influence the way in which an organization tackles self-assessment, for example: the size and resources of the organization, its prevailing culture, its reasons for conducting self-assessment and the progress already made towards self-assessment. In Chapter 3 five broad approaches to self-assessment are examined and the pros and cons of each are discussed.

Whichever approach to self-assessment is adopted the fundamentals of self-assessment remain the same: senior management support and involvement; a clear plan of action; good people with the right skills and resources to make it happen; everyone is aware of what is going on. Chapter 4 looks at practicalities and pitfalls of starting a self-assessment programme.

Many companies either adopt the award-simulation approach to self-assessment right from the outset or move to it as their self-assessment programme matures. This involves writing for the business unit or whole organization undertaking the self-assessment a full submission document along the lines of a European Quality Award application. This submission document (called the position report) is the body of evidence which describes the organization (or part of it) in terms of the criteria of the European Business Excellence Model. Having assembled and presented the information in the form of a single document, the management team will have in their possession something unique. Almost certainly, no other document will have described the organization so comprehensively, in such a concise form and in a manner so potentially useful to the management team. It provides the basis for a database of business excellence which can be updated at regular intervals and used to shape and drive an effective value creation strategy.

The operational steps of an award-simulation approach to self-assessment are described in Chapters 5–9: starting with data collection (Chapter 5); then the practicalities of writing the position report (Chapter 6); how the position report is assessed and scored by experts (the Assessor team) trained to identify the organization's strengths and areas for improvement (Chapter 7); followed by the option of a site visit to validate and verify the contents of the position report (Chapter 8); and finally how the findings of the assessor team are fed back for best effect (Chapter 9).

Is the pursuit of business excellence really worth all the effort? Why should the board continue to invest time and effort when the links to cashflow and profitability often remain unclear? Why should shareholders take an interest? Why should employees squeeze an extra 1 per cent improvement when they have already worked what they believe are miracles? If top managers could see the tremendous impact that relatively small changes in key decisions can have on the bottom line, and if everyone in the company understood how they could personally improve profits, the outcome would be a powerful communication tool for making business excellence initiatives more effective. It would link boardroom performance to operating performance, and provide a way of bringing together directors, operations managers and accountants to focus on the real priorities of the business.

The links between business excellence and the bottom line are explored in Chapter 10. The drivers of shareholder value and the impact of business excellence on shareholder returns are discussed. Over 20 per cent of the companies in the FT non-financial index are earning a return on invested capital below the 'no-risk' bond rate – too low to be of any real value to shareholders. Our research of UK listed companies shows that a 1 per cent improvement in seven key sensitivity factors would impact profits by between 20 and 60 per cent overall. The 1 per cent sensitivity factors can be used to guide goal setting throughout the company, providing a common focus for continuous business improvement. Self-assessment against the criteria of the European Business Excellence Model will identify those activities which have the greatest impact on the 1 per cent sensitivity factors.

Planning for business improvement is essentially an ongoing process of defining, prioritizing, organizing, achieving and reviewing world-class targets of business performance. This requires focusing on those areas critical to success through actively listening to the company's principal stakeholders and identifying the performance levels which affect their satisfaction. This entails the development of a balanced scorecard of financial and non-financial performance measures. Chapter 11 examines the links between cause (improvement actions) and effect (on stakeholder satisfaction), and looks at how a balanced value performance scorecard based on the four results criteria of the European Business Excellence Model can be used to improve business improvement strategy planning.

Experience shows that the achievement of world-class performance requires the creation of an effective company-wide framework for continuous improvement. Customer requirements and stakeholder value creation priorities must be transformed into goals for teams and individuals. Processes need to be analysed and objectives agreed at every level and at every step in the value creation chain. In Chapter 12 a structured year-on-year process for continuous improvement is outlined, and the salient activities – including self-assessment – are described.

By way of background, an overview of the European Quality Award process is given in Chapter 13. This chapter also describes how the award scheme and the European Business Excellence Model were evolved. The two other major international quality awards – the Deming Prize and the Malcolm Baldrige National Quality Award – are discussed and compared with the European Quality Award in Chapter 14.

To win the European Quality Award is an internationally recognized pinnacle of achievement. Most companies undertaking, or about to undertake, business excellence self-assessment will probably never apply for an award, but their aim is the same as an award applicant: to be among the best. To be a winner requires a company to perform well against the same underlying criteria; those of the European Business Excellence Model. Chapter 15 considers not only what it takes to win the European Quality Award but also the characteristics which distinguish the top performing companies from the rest. One factor distinguishes the winners from the losers: the ability to learn fast. It concludes with a brief overview of a company self-learning process that will facilitate the development of a holistic approach to achieving business excellence.

This is not a book about theory, nor does it contain any case studies. Its contents are based on the authors' managerial and academic experiences over the past five or so years which result first, from their early involvement with the European Foundation for Quality Management where they helped to develop the European Business Excellence Model, and then, from their subsequent consultancy practice. It offers down-to-earth guidance to help you to understand business excellence self-assessment, to manage its implementation effectively, and how to use it to identify real, consistent and relevant initiatives to improve business performance and increase stakeholder satisfaction.

Acknowledgements

We would like to acknowledge our many friends and colleagues who encouraged us to write this book and supported us in doing so.

We especially thank our fellow Paragon Directors, David Pentecost and Stan Hedley, for their valuable contributions and patience. Also a Paragon founding director, Chris Brown, whose early proofreading and editing kept us going. David, Chris and Stan were especially influential in the writing of Chapters 3, 7 and 8, respectively.

We are also indebted to our colleague, Geoff Smith, whose thinking on created value and the links between business excellence and financial performance has been crucial to our work in using the European Business Excellence Model as a strategic performance improvement tool. The results of our work with Geoff are especially evident in Chapters 10 and 11.

Thanks are also due to Cathy Paddock, Bill Bowyer, Malcolm Brereton and Vince Grant, who provided many invaluable hints on improving the manuscript.

Our heartfelt thanks go to two people at the sharp end of the production process: Jean McCord, who typed the manuscript as well as fulfilling the demanding role of Paragon's company secretary, and Mitchell Peacock who, under difficult circumstances, managed the graphics.

We also acknowledge the help given by the European Foundation for Quality Management and the VI Group Ltd.

1

Why assess business excellence?

What makes a top performing (or world class) company? Independent studies show that the top performers are those companies which demonstrate consistent, measurable positive business results based on a philosophy of continuous improvement and a capacity to deal with constant change.

From such studies a typical profile of world class performers includes the following characteristics:

- strong leadership
- motivated employees
- extremely high customer satisfaction ratings
- a strong and/or rapidly growing market share
- highly admired by peer group companies and society at large
- business results that put it in the upper quartile of shareholder value.

These may be regarded as characteristics of business excellence.

To achieve business excellence companies need to become learning organizations. Business excellence also demands the following:

- farsighted, committed and involved leaders
- a clear understanding of the company's critical business success factors
- unambiguous direction setting
- flexible and responsive process management
- people with relevant know-how and skill sets
- constant searching to improve the way things are done
- objective assessments of current and future performance.

Top performing companies have learned how to make continuous improvement an integral part of their policy and strategy of business excellence. They have developed a holistic approach based on customer satisfaction and the creative use of the talents of their employees, which has led to financial success.

This book focuses on how companies can best make objective assessments of current and future performance, and how they can use the findings of such assessments to devise and implement an effective strategy for achieving business excellence. In other words, it describes how companies can learn to recognize and pursue business excellence within their own business context and culture.

Becoming tomorrow's excellent company

Although worldwide competition in the 1990s is fierce and getting fiercer, today only a handful of companies can be truly described as 'excellent' or 'world class'. However, excellence is likely to be the hallmark of the successful business organization in the 21st century. In the 21st century there will be many excellent companies; these will be the maturing exponents of Total Quality in its varied forms. Whereas today excellence is so unusual it stands out, in ten years' time excellence will be taken for granted. It will be the expected level of performance – the entry ticket without which an organization will not be a competitor let alone a possible winner.

If you think this is fanciful, consider the impact of Japan on the dynamics of world trade during the past 20 years and on the Total Quality movement. Then consider the likely impact of the emerging economic powerhouse of China; already the first ripples can be seen on the surface. Not to mention what might happen when the Indian subcontinent wakes from its slumber. The traditional notion of business success – better financial performance achieved *somehow* – will on its own be insufficient to survive this onslaught on world markets.

Tomorrow's excellent company will have a wider definition of business success, one that will cover the following issues:

- What we do for our shareholders – investors; generate cash and grow equity
- What we do for our customers – the source of earned cash; revenue growth
- How we do it – be a low cost operating business; improve profits
- How we expand and use our intellectual capital – skills, time, effort and know-how of people
- How our strategies create value for customers and suppliers
- How we make effective use of the financial assets base
- How we recognize the impacts on and of society by creating employment and customers.

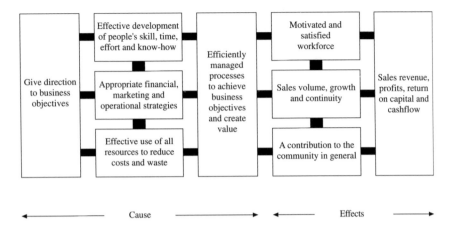

Figure 1.1   An inclusive approach to business excellence

This is an inclusive (or holistic) approach to business excellence (see Fig. 1.1).

While all companies strive for business success, world-class companies aim for excellence and its recognition. Truly world-class companies believe that if they are to remain at the top in tomorrow's competitive environment they must also concentrate on the factors that drive business success: customer satisfaction – how business success is achieved; the effective use of intellectual capital (people); and on the business's role in and impact on society at large. All are equally tangible measures of business success. To quote the RSA's interim report on the 'Tomorrow's Company' inquiry:[1]

> In an inclusive approach success is not defined in terms of a single bottom line, nor is purpose confined to the needs of a single stakeholder. Each company makes its own unique choice of purpose and values, and has its own model of critical business processes from which it derives its range of success measures. But tomorrow's company will understand and measure the value which it derives from all its key relationships, and thereby make informed decisions when it has to balance and trade off the conflicting claims of customers, suppliers, employees, investors and the communities in which it operates.
>
> We believe that to achieve sustainable success tomorrow's company must take an inclusive approach.

Excellent companies do two things:

1. They focus on creating value above all else.
2. They make the right decisions to create value.

The best companies outperform the FT Non-Financial or Dow-Jones indices because they pursue value above all else. When they speak of value they do not mean just financial value. They recognize and work to add value for each of their principal stakeholders:

- *Customers* are offered a product or service that meets, and possibly exceeds, their expectations.
- *Employees* are able to work in an environment where people can progress, where they are respected and their contributions are valued.
- *Shareholders* gain share price appreciation and dividends over time.

Satisfying the requirements of each of these three stakeholders leads to business excellence. Sustained business excellence ensures continued business success.

If you think this is idealistic then consider the words of one of the most successful – and arguably one of the most 'hard-nosed' – business leaders of recent decades, Jack Welch, CEO of General Electric (USA):[2]

> The three most important things you need to measure in a business are Customer Satisfaction, Employee Satisfaction and Cash Flow. If you are growing Customer Satisfaction, your global market share is sure to grow too. Employee Satisfaction gets you productivity, quality, pride and creativity. Cash Flow is the pulse – the vital sign of a company.
>
> We are trying to differentiate GE competitively by raising as much intellectual and creative capital from our workforce as we possibly can. That is a lot tougher than raising financial capital, which a strong company can find in any market in the world.

There is actually a fourth principal stakeholder for whom tomorrow's excellent company must add value if it is to retain its 'franchise' to operate in an ever-turbulent world marketplace: society at large. Business organizations are increasingly being held accountable by the society – both global and local – in which they operate and which they serve. Thus the fourth category of added value can be described as follows:

- *Society* enjoys greater economic wealth, employment and a beneficial impact on the community and on the environment.

For tomorrow's excellent company the route to business success will be in creating value for all four of its principal stakeholders.

Total quality

While business excellence is very much based on the principles and philosophy of Total Quality, its scope is much wider than Total Quality.

Total Quality Management (TQM) evolved out of the manufacturing-related disciplines of quality control and quality assurance, albeit with influences from the service sector with its focus on customer care. Therefore, in the 1980s, a lot of the emphasis was on ISO 9000 and improvement techniques such as statistical process control. With its technical bias, TQM was regarded by most business commentators as a technique or system.

Certainly, as recently as 1990, TQM was still perceived by many experts as a separate management discipline rather than as a management philosophy based on a wider body of knowledge. Much of the debate within the TQM movement in the late 1980s revolved around the need to integrate TQM into the mainstream of business strategy and finding ways of doing so.

There are plenty of business commentators who are critical of TQM. They argue that TQM has failed to deliver the hoped-for results; that it has been internally focused, lacking a clear link to customers or business results; that, at best, it has led only to incremental improvements.

If the surveys carried out by management consultants in the early 1990s are anything to go by, formal TQM programmes do not appear to have had much impact on business performance. McKinsey & Company found that two out of three quality improvement programmes in place for 'more than a couple of years' had stagnated and no longer met senior management expectations for tangible improvement in product or service quality, customer satisfaction, or operating performance. The findings of a survey by Arthur D. Little of 500 US companies indicated that only a third felt that their TQM programmes were having a 'significant impact on their competitiveness'.

The evidence against TQM may, in some quarters, appear pretty damning, but the truth is that many organizations have had unrealistic expectations of TQM and poorly focused initiatives. Often TQM has been perceived as a once-and-for-all panacea for all corporate ills, involving initiatives aimed at changing organizational culture without proper regard for the real issues that drive the business. In many cases TQM programmes were concerned simply with setting the conditions for improvement, tackling the means to the end – raising awareness, mass training, tweaking the organizational structure, unrelated improvement projects – rather than with working towards a clear business improvement strategy.

There is clear evidence, accumulated over the past 10 years, that the core values of TQM, framed within a few simple principles of good management practice, can and have brought about significant impacts on business performance for those organizations with a clear sense of purpose. ICL, Milliken, Rank Xerox and Rover, to name just a few, have all used TQM to help them draw back from the precipice of crisis and not only to survive, but also to go on to regain their competitive edge and prosper. Motorola claims that through TQM it has generated an extra $800 million of revenue during the period 1988–93.

Those organizations that have made TQM work to their competitive advantage have adopted its values and woven them into the fabric of their business. They have not treated TQM as a stand-alone programme or simply as a handy toolkit.

To quote the authors of The Economist Intelligence Unit's report[3]

> The (study) companies agree that TQM is concerned with continuous improvement in performance, aimed at delighting customers: it is much more than the incremental improvement or problem-solving tools and techniques with which it is sometimes associated. To achieve continuous improvement, companies need a holistic approach to change: focusing on customers and practising fact-based management and creating an environment in which people bring to work the same energy, ability and commitment that they display in their life outside work. For most organisations, this means a steep change in approach and culture.

Good management practice

Arguably, TQM is little more than good management practice; albeit a holistic approach to good management. It is, however, a particular definition of good management. The three following emphases differentiate TQM from basic good management practice:

- *It is customer driven.* This means: finding out the customer's expectations; transmitting these throughout the organization as a set of operating objectives; ensuring that these objectives are always met; maintaining customer contact; and recognizing that customer expectations do not remain static.
- *It is concerned with improving processes.* To meet the requirements of a customer-driven business it is necessary to build bridges between functions to create process streams that will behave as added-value chains. This means more than breaking down barriers between functions. To be relevant, process improvement depends on developing a process view of the business around facts-based management; ensuring that people speak with data and are able to identify and resolve the root causes of problems. Process improvement focuses on all organizational processes, including managerial ones.
- *It is concerned with people.* Not just motivating and enriching the jobs of individuals and teams, but building a 'learning organization' in which everyone has the skills, the means and the opportunity to contribute continuously to the creation of added value to the business. This can

mean fundamental changes to the way in which an organization is managed – by values rather than by control. It also means developing a culture in which people are encouraged constantly to develop their skills and self-confidence.

However, good management practice is not as common as one would expect. In fact, the above define *excellent* management – and excellent management is the prime factor that divides the winners from the losers. In essence, business excellence is based not so much on *management of total quality* but on the *total quality of management*.

An inclusive framework for change

The total quality of a management can be judged on how well they are able to manage change effectively – their decision-making and leadership capabilities – and on whether they are creating real value for all of their stakeholders.

Certainly, in the 1990s, new competitive pressures, market dynamics, the relentless pull of technological change and the information revolution have combined to force managers constantly to cope with and facilitate change. The problem is that change is often initiated out of context, without any framework for reference to help determine which change initiatives will add value. To quote a newspaper interview with James Champy,[4] one of the pioneers of the business process re-engineering movement:

> Radical change is impossible unless managers know how to ... organise, inspire, deploy, enable, measure and reward the value adding operational work. The lack of these skills has been a stumbling block to nearly every re-engineering initiative.

Not all change initiatives are major re-engineering projects, in fact most are concerned with incremental improvements. But, whether radical or incremental, all change initiatives must impact positively on business performance. Hitherto, the lack of an inclusive framework for managing change has meant that companies have tended to introduce a never-ending stream of improvement initiatives, often without any overall strategy or any clear idea of how business performance will be affected. Worse still, many executives seem unsure about just which factors drive business success in their companies.

By clearly displaying the links between cause and effect, the European Business Excellence Model (Fig. 1.2) provides an inclusive framework for managing change to best effect. The model, which is used as the basis of both the European and UK Quality Awards, is a flowchart of how an excellent company operates.

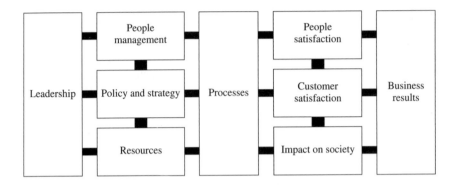

Figure 1.2 The European Business Excellence Model
(*Source:* EFQM)

Developed in 1990–91 by the European Foundation for Quality Management (EFQM), the model is based on the simple premise that processes are the means by which a company harnesses and releases the talents and potential of its people to produce results.

> Customer Satisfaction, People Satisfaction, Impact on Society are achieved through Leadership driving Policy and Strategy, People Management, Resources and Processes leading ultimately to excellence in Business Results.

The logic is simple: by improving the 'how' of a company's operations (the *enablers* of leadership, policy and strategy, people management, resources and processes) improved *results* will follow for each of its key stakeholders (financial, customers, people and society).

There is plenty of evidence that the European Business Excellence Model is fulfilling its intended role of providing managers with a leadership map to help them navigate the contours of business excellence. Companies such as Rank Xerox, ICL, Rover, BT, The Post Office, TNT Express and Glaxo are using the model to help them better understand their own organizations and on what they need to focus to achieve business excellence.

Creating value

How do companies achieve excellence? Earlier we stated that excellent companies focus on creating value above all else and on making the right decisions to create value. In other words, not only are they able to identify and measure the factors which satisfy their key stakeholders (financial, customers, people and society), but they also know where to focus their change initiatives for maximum impact on stakeholder satisfaction.

In very simple terms, the basis of business is to create value by supplying goods and services to customers in return for money. To do so, all businesses use two main resources: intellectual capital (people's skill, time, effort and know-how) and financial capital (fixed or working).

This approach uses a basic concept: sales revenue equates to the income from goods and services that have perceived value and benefits for customers. From sales revenue are deducted the expenditure costs of bought-in materials, supplies and services that have a perceived value to the buyer. The difference between sales revenue and expenditure costs represents the created value to pay for the cost of intellectual capital and financial capital (see Fig. 1.3). Only when all the costs of materials, supplies and services, intellectual capital and financial capital have been met has any real additional value been created by the company.

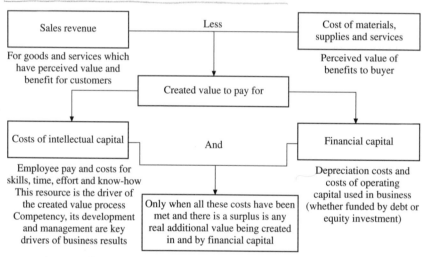

Figure 1.3   The created value concept

The created value concept relates to the following six criteria of the European Business Excellence Model:

- Sales revenue   Customer satisfaction
- Cost of materials,   Process management
  suppliers and services   Resource management

– Cost of intellectual   People management
  capital   People satisfaction
– Financial capital   Resource management
                             Business results

The relationship is shown in Fig. 1.4.

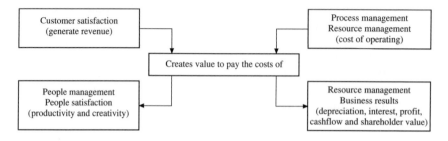

Figure 1.4   How created value relates to the European Business Excellence Model (1)

Figure 1.5 shows the relationship when we add the other three criteria of the European Business Excellence Model. Hence creating value for a company can be achieved by focusing on the nine criteria of the European Business Excellence Model.

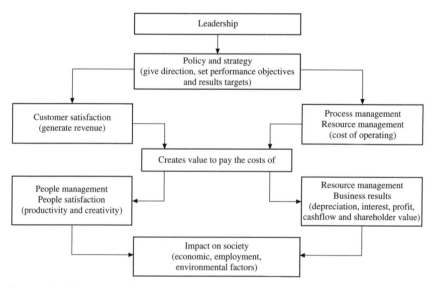

Figure 1.5   How created value relates to the European Business Excellence Model (2)

Making the right decisions

Too few companies manage or prioritize the many change initiatives that occur throughout their organizations. Moreover, few analyse their total activities on a regular basis to identify opportunities for improvement. However, the critical business priorities can readily be identified and managed using a self-assessment process based on the European Business Excellence Model. To quote the EFQM's self-assessment guidelines: 'Self-assessment is a comprehensive, systematic and regular review of an organization's activities and results referenced against a model of business excellence.'

The self-assessment process allows the organization to identify clearly, under each of the nine criteria, its strengths and areas in which improvements can be made. It is an exercise which can be done annually to benchmark and review an organization's overall business activities and how they impact on its stakeholders. It can enhance management's strategic decision-making capacity by identifying those activities and opportunities that have the greatest impact on created value. In other words, it helps answer that nagging question of management: 'Are we taking the right actions to produce the right results?'

Self-assessment also allows management more confidently to answer the question: 'What do we have to do to improve our results?' The information generated by the exercise is an invaluable input to strategic planning, and enables the senior management team to create a business improvement strategy focused on the priorities that have greatest impact on stakeholder value (see Fig. 1.6).

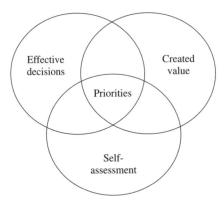

Figure 1.6 Linking self-assessment to created value

Self-assessment based on the European Business Excellence Model provides the senior management team with several keys to understanding the following:

- how your company works
- how good you are
- how you compare with others
- how good you need (want) to be
- what needs changing
- how to get started.

The beauty of self-assessment is that it really does help you learn how to build tomorrow's excellent company, *today*.

References

1. Royal Society of Arts. *Tomorrow's Company: The role of business in a changing world*, Interim Report, RSA, London, 1994.
2. 'Jack Welch's Lessons for Success', *Fortune*, 25 January 1993, p. 68.
3. Binney, G. *Making Quality Work : Lessons from Europe's leading companies*, The Economist Intelligence Unit, London, 1992.
4. Dickson, T. 'Executive heal thyself', *Financial Times*, 10 February 1995.

2
The European Business Excellence Model

To undertake a self-assessment of business excellence, you need an inclusive, well-ordered (but not too prescriptive) framework. An ideal framework is The European Model for Total Quality Management, increasingly called the European Business Excellence Model. Although each organization is unique, this model provides a generic framework of criteria that can be applied widely to any organization or component part of an organization.

This chapter describes the structure of the model, highlights its constituent parts and outlines the assessment scoring system.

The structure of the model

The basis of the model, developed by the EFQM, is the achievement of good *results* through the involvement of all employees (the *people*) in continuous improvement of their *processes* (see Fig. 2.1).

Figure 2.1 Simple improvement model
(*Source:* EFQM)

This simple model was expanded into the European Business Excellence Model which provides the framework for both company self-assessment and the European Quality Award (and for the United Kingdom and other national quality awards in Europe).

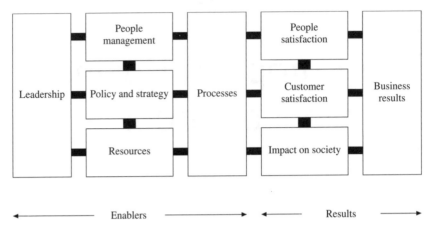

Figure 2.2   The European business excellence criteria
(*Source:* EFQM)

The model is structured on nine criteria against which companies can assess and measure their own excellence and target continuous improvement, as shown in Fig. 2.2. The criteria are as follows:

1. *Leadership*: the behaviour of all managers in driving the company towards business excellence. How the executive team and all other managers inspire and drive excellence as the organization's fundamental process for continuous improvement.
2. *Policy and strategy*: the organization's values, vision and strategic direction and the manner in which it achieves them. How the organization incorporates the concept of excellence in the determination, communication, implementation, review and improvement of its policy and strategy.
3. *People management*: the management of the organization's people. How the organization releases the full potential of its people to improve its business continuously.
4. *Resources*: the management, utilization and preservation of resources. How the organization improves its business continuously by optimization of resources, based on the concept of excellence.
5. *Processes*: the management of all the value-adding activities within the organization. How key and support processes are identified, reviewed and if necessary revised to ensure continuous improvement of the organization's business.
6. *Customer satisfaction*: the perception of the external customers, direct and indirect, of the organization and of its products and services. The

organization's success in satisfying the needs and expectations of customers.

7. *People satisfaction*: the people's (employees) feelings about the organization. The organization's success in satisfying the needs and expectations of its people.

8. *Impact on society*: the perception of the organization among the community at large. This includes views of the organization's approach to quality of life, to the environment and to the preservation of global resources. It is about the organization's success in satisfying the needs and expectations of the community at large.

9. *Business results*: what the organization is achieving in relation to its planned business performance. The organization's continuing success in achieving its financial and other business targets and objectives and in satisfying the needs and expectations of everyone with a financial interest in the organization.

The flow of the model can be summarized quite simply as follows:

Customer Satisfaction, People Satisfaction, Impact on Society are achieved through Leadership driving Policy and Strategy, People Management, Resources and Processes leading ultimately to excellence in Business Results.

In essence the model is a leadership map of how an excellently managed business organization operates – and that is its primary strength.

The model's second great strength is the way the criteria are split between cause and effect. The five criteria on the left-hand side of the model are *enablers*, and are concerned with *how* things are done through the management approaches that are in place. The four criteria on the right are *results*, and these are concerned with *what* has, and is being, achieved from the viewpoint of four key stakeholders: the customers, the organization's own people, society and those with a financial investment in the business.

The percentages shown in each box of Fig. 2.3 indicate the weighting given to each criterion in the scoring system (see Chapter 7). The percentages allocated to each criterion were established following a wide-ranging exercise to collect views from business leaders, practitioners, academics and consultants (see Chapter 13). Customer satisfaction has the highest weighting at 20 per cent, people management and satisfaction together are 18 per cent, business results 15 per cent, and so on. Notice that the percentages allocated to the criteria ensure that 50 per cent of the weight is attributed to enablers and 50 per cent to results. Thus to score highly an organization must be able to demonstrate not only excellent management

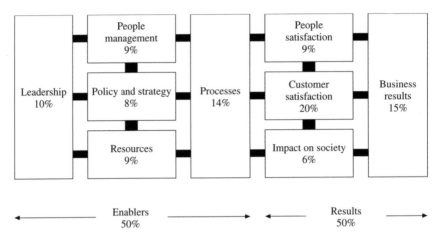

Figure 2.3 The excellence criteria weightings
(*Source:* EFQM)

approaches but also that these approaches have had a significant beneficial impact on the stakeholders of the business.

The criteria weights shown in Fig. 2.3 reflect the current (1996) European Quality Award scoring system, and have not changed since the award's launch in 1991. They represent a view of an excellently managed business organization some five years into the future.

As events unfold, the EFQM may decide to refine individual criterion weightings in the light of developing information and changing conditions – for example, the weighting for impact on society could conceivably increase in the future. But any refinement of the scoring system will take place only after extensive consultation with all the European national quality organizations and will be very gradual in nature. The model will continue to reflect a view of tomorrow's company.

Each criterion is divided into several parts. Each part is concerned with a specific salient issue. For example, leadership is divided into six parts (a to f). Part (a) deals with the visible involvement of managers; part (b) is about managers developing a consistent total quality culture; part (c) is about recognition and appreciation; part (d) involves the support for total quality within the organization; part (e), the involvement of managers with customers and suppliers; and part (f), the active promotion of total quality outside the organization. The parts within enabler criteria all have equal weighting (see Fig. 2.4).

The areas to address for each criterion part are non-prescriptive. Both the EFQM[1] and BQF[2] publish 'guidelines', but these are not intended as an

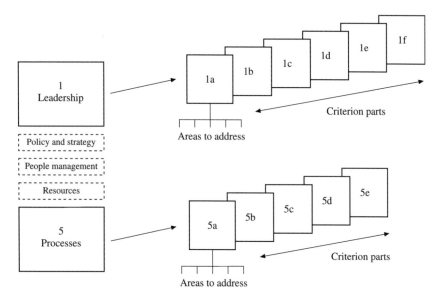

Figure 2.4   Breakdown of enabler criteria
(*Source:* EFQM)

exhaustive check-list. It is up to organizations using the model for self-assessment to interpret the areas to address as appropriate to their business context.

In fact, the BQF's 1996 self-assessment guidelines document contains a second set of areas to address for business results adapted to suit 'not-for-profit' organizations. The model's third great strength is that it is a non-prescriptive model which can be adopted by varying business cultures.

Results criteria are each divided into two parts, but not all are equally weighted – see 'The criteria for excellence' in the following section and in the appendix. In common with the enablers, the guidelines for the results criterion parts are non-prescriptive.

Assessment of results criteria is based on the evidence of trends of actual results and comparisons of those trends with both internal and external measures. The external measures should be for competitors and selected best-in-class organizations. Trends are used to avoid looking at just a snapshot in time of the organization's performance. Trends over a period of at least three years, and preferably five or more, are needed to score highly.

The criteria for excellence

Enablers

1. LEADERSHIP

The behaviour of all managers in driving the organization towards Total Quality.

How the executive team and all other managers inspire and drive Total Quality as the organization's fundamental process for continuous improvement.

Evidence is needed of:

1a. Visible involvement in leading Total Quality
1b. A consistent Total Quality culture
1c. Timely recognition and appreciation of the efforts and successes of individuals and teams
1d. Support of Total Quality by provision of appropriate resources and assistance
1e. Involvement with customers and suppliers
1f. The active promotion of Total Quality outside the organization.

(Each criterion part takes an equal share of the points allocated to criterion 1.)

2. POLICY AND STRATEGY

The organization's mission, values, vision and strategic direction – and the manner in which it achieves them.

How the organization's policy and strategy reflects the concept of Total Quality and how the principles of Total Quality are used in the formulation, deployment, review and improvement of policy and strategy.

Evidence is needed of how policy and strategy are:

2a. Formulated on the concept of Total Quality
2b. Based on information that is relevant and comprehensive
2c. The basis for business plans
2d. Communicated
2e. Regularly updated and improved.

(Each criterion part takes an equal share of the points allocated to criterion 2.)

3. PEOPLE MANAGEMENT

The management of the organization's people.

How the organization releases the full potential of its people to improve its business continuously.

Evidence is needed of how:

3a. People resources are planned and improved
3b. The skills and capabilities of the people are preserved and developed through recruitment, training and career progression
3c. People and teams agree targets and continuously review performance
3d. The involvement of everyone in continuous improvement is promoted and people are empowered to take appropriate action
3e. Effective top-down and bottom-up communication is achieved.

(Each criterion part takes an equal share of the points allocated to criterion 3.)

4. RESOURCES

The management, utilization and preservation of resources.

How the organization's resources are effectively deployed in support of policy and strategy.

Evidence is needed of how business improvements are achieved continuously by the management of:

4a. Financial resources
4b. Information resources
4c. Suppliers, materials, buildings and equipment
4d. The application of technology.

(Each criterion part takes an equal share of the points allocated to criterion 4.)

5. PROCESSES

The management of all value-adding activities within the organization.

How processes are identified, reviewed and if necessary revised to ensure continuous improvement of the organization's business.

Evidence is needed of how:

5a. Processes critical to the success of the business are identified (including a list of critical processes)
5b. The organization systematically manages its processes
5c. Process performance measurements, along with all relevant feedback

are used to review processes and to set targets for improvement

5d. The organization stimulates innovation and creativity in process improvement

5e. The organization implements process changes and evaluates the benefits.

(Each criterion part takes an equal share of the points allocated to criterion 5.)

Results

6. CUSTOMER SATISFACTION

What the organization is achieving in relation to the satisfaction of its external customers.

Evidence is needed of:

6a. The customer's perception of the organization's products, services and customer relationships

6b. Additional measures relating to the satisfaction of the organization's customers.

(Criterion part 6a accounts for 75 per cent of the points and criterion part 6b 25 per cent of the points available.)

7. PEOPLE SATISFACTION

What the organization is achieving in relation to satisfaction of its people.

Evidence is needed of:

7a. The people's perception of the organization

7b. Additional measures relating to people satisfaction.

(Criterion part 7a accounts for 75 per cent of the points and criterion part 7b 25 per cent of the points available.)

8. IMPACT ON SOCIETY

What the organization is achieving in satisfying the needs and the expectations of the community at large. This includes perceptions of the organization's approach to quality of life, to the environment and to the preservation of the global resources and the organization's own internal measures.

Evidence is needed of:

8a. The perception of the community at large of the organization's impact on society

8b. Additional measures relating to the organization's impact on society.

(Criterion part 8a accounts for 25 per cent of the points and criterion part 8b 75 per cent of the points available.)

9. BUSINESS RESULTS

What the organization is achieving in relation to its planned business performance and in satisfying the needs and expectations of everyone with a financial interest in the organization.

Evidence is needed of:

9a. Financial measures of the organization's success

9b. Non-financial measures of the organization's success.

(Each criterion part takes an equal share of the points allocated to criterion 9.)

Scoring excellence

Any company or business unit – or for that matter 'not-for-profit' organization – can assess itself against the criteria of the European Business Excellence Model using the assessment scoring system devised for the European Quality Award. This assessment scoring system is also the basis for the UK Quality Award and an increasing number of other national and regional quality awards in Europe.

The assessors allocate percentage points for the organization's performance against each of the criterion parts of the model. Different, but complementary, factors are used to evaluate enablers and results.

Enablers

Each of the parts of the enabler criteria are evaluated according to approach and deployment.

Approach is concerned with the methods the organization uses to address the criterion parts. The score given takes account of the following:

– the appropriateness of the methods, tools and techniques
– the degree to which the approach is systematic and prevention based
– the use of review cycles
– the implementation of improvements resulting from review cycles
– the degree to which the approach has been integrated into normal operations.

Deployment is concerned with the extent to which the approach has been implemented to its full potential. The score given takes account of appropriate and effective application of the approach as follows:

- vertically through all relevant levels
- horizontally through all relevant areas and activities
- in all relevant processes
- to all relevant products and services.

Results

The *excellence* of results take account of the following:

- the existence of positive trends
- comparisons with own targets
- comparisons with external organizations including competitors and 'best in class' organizations
- the organization's ability to sustain its performance
- indications that results are caused by appropriate approaches.

The *scope* of results takes account of the following:

- the extent to which the results cover all relevant areas of the organization
- the extent to which a full range of results, relevant to the criterion part, are presented
- the extent to which the relevance of the results is understood.

A discussion of the assessment scoring and consensus processes can be found in Chapter 7.

References

1. European Foundation for Quality Management. *Self-assessment 1996 Guidelines*, EFQM, Brussels.
2. British Quality Foundation. *Self-assessment 1996 Guidelines*, BQF, London.

3
Doing self-assessment

There are several ways in which you may implement self-assessment in your organization. Self-assessment is not intended as a rigid system – far from it. It was developed as a simple diagnostic technique to support and complement an organization's own business improvement strategy.

Various factors may influence the way in which an organization tackles self-assessment, for example:

- size and resources of the organization
- the culture of the organization
- the planned role of self-assessment in the organization
- progress already made towards self-assessment.

There are several approaches to self-assessment, many of which are described in the EFQM[1] and BQF[2] self-assessment guidelines. They are not entirely separate and combinations can be tried. Much depends on the company's objectives for the exercise. But, generally, the more you put in, the more you will get out of the process. The broad approaches are as follows:

- Award simulation
- Peer involvement
- Workshop
- Matrix chart
- Questionnaire.

Approaches to self-assessment

Award simulation

This approach involves writing for the business unit or whole organization undertaking the self-assessment a full submission document (up to 75 pages is allowed) along the lines described in *The European Quality Award*[3] and *UK Quality Award*[4] *Application Brochures*. An internal process similar to that employed in the award is then established using a team of trained assessors. For a business unit the assessors can originate from another business unit of the organization. If the whole organization is involved some external assessors can be used.

A typical process includes the following steps:

1. The management team of the business or service unit in question agrees to undertake a self-assessment using the written report approach.
2. A project manager is appointed to manage the complete process, including the role of report architect – the person who pulls the report together into its final format.
3. Members of the management team take responsibility for one or more specific criteria and appropriate personnel are identified to be members of a report writing team.
4. The report writing team undergoes training.
5. The report writing team gathers data and compiles sections of the report.
6. The report architect compiles the final version.
7. The report writers give a presentation to the senior manager.
8. The senior manager accepts the report as a fair representation of the business/service unit.
9. Copies of the report are sent to the individual members of the assessor team.
10. The assessors individually identify the strengths and areas for improvement and score the report.
11. The assessors, led by the senior assessor, reach consensus and produce a feedback report, including resolution of 'site visit' issues, which is achieved by contacting the project manager for clarification.
12. The assessors give a presentation to the management team of the business/service unit being assessed.
13. The management team prioritizes the strengths and areas for improvement.
14. The management team agrees ownership and action plans.
15. The management team monitors action plans regularly during the 12-month period between self-assessments. The process is repeated annually to ensure continuous improvement.

Peer involvement

This approach has many similarities to award simulation but allows the business unit undertaking the self-assessment complete freedom in putting together in the 'submission', which may at one extreme be a set of existing documents, reports, graphs, etc. and at the other be something very close to a genuine award application document.

The approach combines extensive involvement from within the unit with a contribution from trained assessors drawn from managers external to the unit. Their role is to help the unit see itself objectively, not arbitrarily to judge, advise or consult.

Typically, this approach includes the following steps:

1. An executive workshop for the business unit's management team to familiarize them with the process and establish roles and responsibilities. During the workshop an executive from another business unit or an external consultant facilitates the management team through a simple self-scoring exercise to generate an initial indication of performance against the European Business Excellence Model.
2. The business unit collects data relevant to the criteria of the model. The format in which the data is presented for assessment can vary from company to company. Some companies insist on a formal award-style position report; some use a detailed questionnaire; some produce a set of one-page pro formas for each criterion part; others simply assemble and categorize existing documents and information.
3. The data collected is reviewed by a team of trained assessors drawn from other business units, perhaps supplemented by an external manager or consultant.
4. The assessor team conducts a site visit. This visit may take three days. On the first day the assessors meet with the executive team to gain an overall understanding of the major policies, strategies and approaches and key results for the unit. On the second day the assessors meet with small groups of senior and middle management to explore the programmes and processes in place to support the overall approaches. On the third day the assessors run facilitated discussion groups with randomly invited groups of employees to gain their perspective of the business unit. The result of this visit is a 'data picture' of the business unit drawn from all parts of the organization (see Fig. 3.1).
5. The assessors spend a day individually assessing the unit's 'Data Picture' against the Business Excellence Model. On the final day the assessor team meets and goes through a consensus process to agree a team view on the strengths, areas for improvement and scores for the business unit.
6. The assessor team prepares a report listing key strengths, areas for improvement and scores. This is sent to each member of the unit's management team.
7. The assessor team meet with the business unit's executive team to discuss the report.

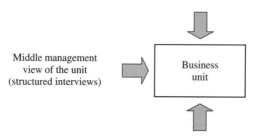

Executive team view of the unit
(executive workshop and executive team interviews)

Middle management
view of the unit
(structured interviews)

Business
unit

Other views of the unit
(discussion groups, involving other
people employed by the organization)

Figure 3.1   Peer involvement data picture
(*Source:* EFQM/Royal Mail)

8. The contents of the feedback report is converted by the business unit's management team into an action plan.
9. The process is repeated periodically, usually after 12 months.

Workshop

This is a management-led approach where, after some preliminary training, managers are responsible for gathering the data and presenting the evidence to their peers at a scoring workshop. During the workshop a consensus score is reached by the management team and a list of strengths and areas for improvement are agreed.

A typical process involves the following steps:

1. The management team attends a one-day training workshop. This begins with around three hours of preparatory reading of an EFQM training case study extract before attending the workshop. Typically the workshop covers an overview of the European Business Excellence Model criteria and scoring system, case study work and a brief simulation of the scoring workshop to be held approximately four/six weeks later.
2. The members of the management team individually gather the data with the help of their reportees. Data gathering can be an early learning opportunity for the management team. Sufficient time needs to be allowed for this task.
3. The management team meets for a scoring workshop. This is a demanding event requiring at least a full day or possibly one-and-a-

half days for its completion. The two workshop facilitators help the management team work through all 33 criterion parts of the European Business Excellence Model.

A common process is followed for all 33 criterion parts:
- A criterion part is described by a member of the management team.
- Information gathered beforehand is presented to other members of the team in the form of strengths and areas for improvement.
- A check is made with the rest of the team to see if anything has been missed out that has relevance to the criterion part.
- There is a discussion and agreement on strengths and areas for improvement.
- Team members score individually.
- Individual scores are shared.
- Consensus is gained.

Experience shows that two people, fully trained as assessors, are required to facilitate the process. They should be from outside the company or business unit.

4. The management team reconvene approximately one to two weeks later for an action planning workshop to agree improvement priorities and plans, based on the output of the scoring workshop.
5. Progress against the action plans are reviewed as part of the normal business review progress.
6. The data collection, scoring workshop and action planning workshop processes are repeated at appropriate intervals as part of an ongoing continuous improvement strategy.

Matrix chart

This approach involves the use of a company-specific achievement matrix based on the European Business Excellence Model. The matrix typically consists of a series of statements of achievements on a points scale of 1 to 10 or similar. Levels of achievement are designated by an ascending order of statements against each criterion of the model. An example is shown in Fig. 3.2.

The matrix chart approach can be used at any level within the company, either by the management team or by a representative cross-section of the people from the business unit undergoing the self-assessment.

This approach may involve the following steps:

1. A briefing is held to introduce assessment team members to the matrix and clarify expectations of the process. Each team member receives a copy of the achievement matrix, usually included in a workbook, in

STEP	LEADERSHIP	POLICY AND STRATEGY	PEOPLE MANAGEMENT	RESOURCES	PROCESSES
10	All managers are proactive in sustaining continuous improvement.	Mission and business policy statements cover the whole business, and everyone understands them.	All actions are directed towards realizing the full potential of all employees.	The organization's resources are deployed effectively to meet policy and strategy objectives.	Key value-added processes are understood, formally managed and continuously improved.
9	Managers are able to demonstrate their external involvement in the promotion of Total Quality as a business philosophy based on their own experience.	A process is in place to analyse competitor business strategy and to modify unit plans as a result, in order to sustain a competitive advantage.	Employees are empowered to run their business processes.	A process is in place to identify additional resources that can be used to strengthen competitive advantage.	The existence of a formal quality management system can be demonstrated.
8	Managers have a consistent approach towards continuous improvement across the unit.	The policy and strategy processes are benchmarked.	The human resource plan for the unit supports the company's policy and strategy for continuous improvement.	A system is in place to review and modify the allocation of resources based on changing business needs.	Process performance is demonstrably linked to customer requirements.
7	The management team are proactive in valuing, recognizing and rewarding all employees for continuous improvement.	A process is in place to modify policy and strategy as a result of business and operational information.	A process is in place to encourage creativity and innovation among all employees.	A process is in place for identifying, assessing and evaluating new technologies and their impact on the business.	A mechanism is in place for developing and using appropriate measures which evaluate key processes.
6	Managers are visibly involved in the development and support of improvement teams and act as champions.	A process is in place to assess the continuing relevance of plans as a result of business and operational information.	Improvement teams have been established and supported.	Systems are in place to track, monitor and review targeted areas to reduce all other waste including time and rework.	The process results are reviewed and fed back into the improvement cycle.
5	A process is in place to ensure managers are working with customers and suppliers, and that the effectiveness of this process can be assured.	The unit has policy statements and strategy that cover the nine business improvement matrix headings.	Training and development needs are regularly reviewed for all employees and teams. Skill gaps relevant to personal aspirations and business needs are identified.	Systems are in place to track, monitor and review targeted areas to reduce material waste.	An improvement mechanism for key value-added processes has been implemented.
4	A process is in place to ensure managers are visibly involved as role models in business improvement within the unit. The effectiveness of the process is reviewed.	A process exists and is reviewed that promotes a clear understanding of the company's and unit's mission, critical success factor (CSF) and policy statements, so that everyone knows and understands these.	An effective appraisal system is in place for all employees.	A process is in place to manage the dissemination of relevant information to customers, suppliers and employees.	An improvement mechanism has been identified and targets for improvement have been set.
3	A process is in place to ensure mutual understanding of business issues through two-way communication both vertically and horizontally throughout the unit.	A process is in place to collect all the relevant internal information to enable a review of CSFs and business plans.	A process is in place for two-way communication of business information within the unit.	Partnerships with suppliers are being developed jointly to improve quality, delivery and performance.	The effectiveness of existing key value-added processes is assessed.
2	A process is in place to create and continually to increase an open awareness of business issues throughout the unit.	A process is in place to collect relevant internal information to enable a review of CSFs and business plans.	A public commitment has been given to develop all employees to achieve business goals.	A process is in place to identify suppliers for key resources.	Key value-added processes are identified, flowcharted and/or documented. Ownership is established.
1	The management team has a process in place to develop its own awareness of the concepts of Total Quality.	The unit management team has developed a mission statement and CSFs.	A process is in place to canvass and track employee opinion.	A process is in place to identify what resources are available and how they are being deployed.	The main processes within the business unit are identified.

Figure 3.2 Business excellence achievement matrix
(*Source:* British Gas)

RESULTS

STEP	CUSTOMER SATISFACTION	PEOPLE SATISFACTION	IMPACT ON SOCIETY	BUSINESS RESULTS
10	There is a positive trend in customer satisfaction. Targets are being met. There are some benchmarking targets across the industry.	Regular comparison with external companies show employee satisfaction is comparable with other companies and has improving trends.	Views of local society are proactively canvassed. Results are fed back into the company's policies.	There are consistent trends of improvement in 50% of key results areas. Some results are clearly linked to approach.
9	75% of customer satisfaction targets are being met.	Results indicate that employees and their families feel integrated into the work environment.	Benchmarking has started for 25% of impact on society targets.	All targets are being met and showing continuous improvements in 25% of trends.
8	50% of customer satisfaction targets are being met.	Results indicate that people feel valued for their contribution at work.	50% of impact on society targets are being met.	75% of targets have been achieved. Able to demonstrate relevance of key results areas in business.
7	All employees understand targets relating to customer satisfaction.	Results indicate that people can express their feelings confidently and openly.	Results are linked to environmental and social policy. Policy is reviewed.	Performance against others in the industry is compared and targets are reset.
6	The drivers of customer satisfaction have been identified and are used to modify targets.	Targets are set in key improvement areas and are published.	There is an increased public awareness of policies.	Improving and adverse trends have been identified, understood and linked to enablers.
5	Compare customer satisfaction levels within the company. Results have positive trend and some are meeting targets.	Trends are established. Positive and negative trends are understood. Parameters measured are relevant to employees.	There are consistently improving trends in relevant result areas.	50% of internal targets have been met.
4	The relevance of targets to customer satisfaction can be demonstrated.	The effeciveness of two-way internal communication is measured.	Local perception and needs are researched and targets are set for improvement.	Trends are compared against the unit's goals and financial objectives.
3	Targets are set for improvement.	Data is used to plot trends for employee satisfaction.	Employees' awareness of relevant result areas is measured.	Relevant results are communicated to all employees and key results are published regularly.
2	Data is used to plot trends of customer complaints.	Key measures of employee satisfaction have been identified.	Trends are established, and a process is in place to track progress.	A system exists for measuring and monitoring key results areas.
1	Customer complaints are logged, and reacted to on an ad hoc basis.	Employee grievances are reacted to on an ad hoc basis.	Result areas have been identified.	The unit's key financial and non-financial objectives have been identified.

Figure 3.2 *continued*

which they mark their own rating of the unit being assessed. The workbook provides all of the instructions necessary to complete this exercise.

2. Approximately one week later, the team meets for a full-day consensus workshop assisted by a trained facilitator. Although a fully trained assessor, the facilitator's role is not to decide the rating, but to use questioning techniques and facilitation skills to help the team agree on their rating of the unit.

3. Subsequently, there is an action planning meeting in which the assessment team uses their consensus rating and discussion notes as a basis for producing and implementing an action plan for improvement.

4. The consensus workshop is repeated every six to twelve months to help guide a continuous improvement programme.

Questionnaire

This is the simplest approach, varying from a simple yes/no questionnaire based on the criteria, criterion parts and areas to address of the European Business Excellence Model, to a sophisticated set of penetrating questions with a weighting and scoring method.

Some organizations use simple yes/no questionnaires, such as that shown in Fig. 3.3, as a method for widespread data gathering in support of more elaborate self-assessment processes such as the workshop approach.

Leadership	Yes	No
Do the leaders create an environment to achieve success?		
Do the leaders encourage people to contribute ideas, views and opinions?		
Policy and strategy		
Is the policy and strategy of the organization based on feedback from customers and suppliers?		
Does the organization use benchmark performance of competitors and/or 'best in class' to help formulate policy and strategy?		

Figure 3.3 Sample yes/no questionnaire
(*Source:* EFQM)

Other organizations use more sophisticated questionnaires as the prime method for analysing strengths and areas for improvement, and establishing the basis for the business improvement plan. In these questionnaires, multiple choice answers are required rather than yes/no responses. An example is given in Fig. 3.4.

People management	D	C	B	A
Does your organization have a process, which is respected by the people, for regular appraisals, and which includes training and career development needs?				
Have effective two-way communications been achieved with the people, and would they agree that they are well informed and their opinion valued?				

D = Not started   C = Some progress   B = Considerable progress
A = Fully achieved

Figure 3.4   Sample multiple choice questionnaire
(*Source:* EFQM)

Miscellaneous

Two further methods should be mentioned:

1. The creation of a set of pro formas which summarize the evidence for each criterion part on a single form. These are scored by trained assessors. Typically, each pro forma contains a description of the criterion part, a list of the areas to address, and space to add strengths, areas for improvement and evidence. Usually one pro forma is prepared for each criterion part, making 33 in total.

   The pro forma method is not a stand-alone assessment approach. It is always used with one of the other approaches, such as peer involvement or workshops.

2. A variation of the award simulation approach is to write a position report featuring perhaps only two of the nine criteria of the European Business Excellence Model – for example, people management and people satisfaction. Using two or perhaps three criteria as a starting point allows an organization to test a powerful, but resource-hungry approach and to realize some of the benefits on the basis of a more limited data collection capability. Over a period of time this approach can be extended to cover all nine criteria.

Self-assessment approaches compared

Only you can decide which approach is most appropriate for your organization. To help you consider the pros and cons of each approach we have made a brief comparison of all five against seven core assessment-related activities.

Core assessment activities

Figure 3.5 is a flowchart of seven sequential activities, at the heart of the European/UK Quality Award process, which we have selected for the comparison. (This is not the complete range of award-related activities; the support activities and activities concerning, for example, the Award jury, are excluded.)

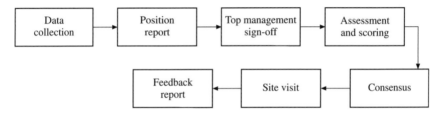

Figure 3.5   Award-style core assessment activities

1. *Data collection* involves the systematic gathering, analysis and collection of information on the organization's approach to managing excellence and its results.
2. The *position report* is the body of evidence on how well the organization is managing business excellence. For an application to the European or UK Quality Award this report is limited in length to 75 pages.
3. *Top management sign-off* of the position report before it is submitted for assessment, indicates senior management's acceptance of its contents as a fair representation of the organization and what is being achieved.
4. *Assessment and scoring* of the position report is done by a team of 6/7 assessors working independently in the first instance.
5. *Consensus* is achieved when the assessor team meets to share individual assessments and produces a composite score and list of strengths, areas for improvement and site visit issues.
6. A *site visit* to the organization enables the assessor team to verify the validity of the position report and clarify any unclear aspects.
7. The *feedback report* contains the findings of the assessment: strengths and

areas for improvement for each criterion part are listed, scores for each criterion are summarized.

Award simulation

DATA COLLECTION

An important and thorough process. A data collection team is set up to collect data. The same team may also carry out the assessment, but usually not. Team members must have been trained in the model and assessment and scoring processes. Data collection can be assisted by check-lists based on the criteria/subcriteria of the model.

POSITION REPORT

This serves the same purpose as an award application, but there may be slight differences. It is written for in-company use only. There is the problem of whether to put only the 'best foot forward' rather than the 'warts and all' version in the report. The data collection team must make a fair summary against each criterion, but there is more scope in a position report than in an award application for gaps in the data, and for avoiding 'gilding' the information. The opposite danger is that the position report becomes too 'customized' to the unit being assessed and loses objectivity. Ways to get round this include the selection of team members from outside the organization and use of check-lists.

MANAGEMENT AGREEMENT

The position report is usually presented to the management team by the data collection team for their agreement before the assessment and scoring is done. The management team may disagree on information given, and suggest areas in which it can be improved. Management must be prepared to down-grade exaggerated claims, as well as to improve 'undersold' features. This process performs, in effect, many of the aspects of a site visit. The management discussion may also confirm the principles and timetable for the assessment and scoring stage.

ASSESSMENT AND SCORING

This is done on the same principles and techniques as for an Award Application. Six or seven assessors are usually chosen, and they must be given training in assessment for the European Business Excellence Model.

The company may change the weighting, but usually does not. Appointment of the team leader, and team selection are important – to get the right people; to have the right spread of background experience and representation of the units covered by the position report; and, if possible, to include an external member. The team must be given time and facilities to do a good job. If it is the same team that collected the data, its task will be shorter than for a new assessor team. But the new assessor team should not normally consult the data collection team, or management, any further once it has commenced its task. The team must judge on the position report alone.

CONSENSUS PROCESS

This is as for an award application. After individual assessments by each team member, the team leader receives the initial strength/areas for improvement and scores. The standard EFQM/BQF scorebook is used by most organizations. The EFQM/BQF rules for when to hold a consensus meeting are also usually applied (i.e., if there are more than 25 percentage points difference on any or all of the criteria). In practice, such meetings are almost always held to review the scores and the strengths/areas for improvement, and to prepare for the feedback report.

SITE VISIT

There is usually no formal site visit as adopted in the EFQM/BQF award application because there is usually no need for verification or clarification at this stage of an internal self-assessment. If the assessor team is the same team as the data collection team, there should be few, if any, issues for clarification. They would probably have been considered when putting the position report together. Where the assessor team is different, there may be more issues listed, and, where necessary in exceptional cases, the team may need to discuss a point for clarification with the senior manager concerned, or the project manager.

FEEDBACK REPORT

This is adapted to the needs of the organization, but because it is drafted by an internal assessor team, it may be less 'judgemental' than an external feedback report (e.g., from BQF or EFQM). It might go into more specific detail, and it might reveal more information on the scores, and comparisons with external benchmarks. There are dangers in allowing the feedback report to be a 'discussion document' between the team and senior management (e.g., undermining scoring variations, credibility of individual members of the team). However, a verbal presentation of the report to senior management is quite usual.

Advantages of the award simulation approach include a high degree of correlation with the European Business Excellence Model and therefore a high level of accuracy and opportunities for external benchmarking. It is the only approach that generates a structured documentary body of evidence that can be regularly updated to form a 'live' business excellence database. It is also necessary if the long-term aim is to apply for an award.

Disadvantages include the length of time and the resources required to complete. Also, management may not be as closely involved in the process as some other methods. 'Cultural' issues (e.g., managerial fear, divisional/ professional barriers, 'not-invented-here' syndrome) may be against a wholesale approach.

Peer involvement

DATA COLLECTION

This is similar to the award simulation approach except that there is no formal procedure for data collection and there is a lot more emphasis on the site visit, taking the form of information gathering and evaluation. Data collection can be anything from a small team collecting existing documentation up to a formal position report. The data collection team is drawn from the unit being assessed, and is given awareness training on the model and the self-assessment evaluation and scoring processes.

POSITION REPORT

There is usually no formal position report. Some preliminary information is collected for the assessor team, covering the areas for investigation in each of the nine criteria of the model.

MANAGEMENT AGREEMENT

This is limited to endorsement of the information going to the assessor team, and the terms under which the team will conduct its site visit.

ASSESSMENT AND SCORING

This is done by the assessor team as a result of their site visit. They may do this individually and then meet for a consensus meeting. Alternatively, the assessment and scoring may be done throughout as a group task. The assessor team is drawn from managers (often senior line managers to give them credibility and authority) who are external to the unit being assessed. They are fully trained in the use of the model.

CONSENSUS PROCESS

This is done by the assessors as a result of the site visit.

SITE VISIT

The role of the senior management assessors goes beyond that of the normal assessor. They help the unit to see itself objectively. They review the data, identify the issues on which they need clarification or more information. During their site visit they meet the executive team of the unit to review its policies, and results. Then they meet with selected groups and individuals in middle management, followed by discussion groups of randomly selected employees. The site visit may last three days and is used to build up a data picture of the unit from which the team then draws up a list of strengths/ areas for improvement.

FEEDBACK REPORT

Following the site visit the assessor team writes a feedback report, and presents this to the management team of the unit being assessed. Because this is a 'peer' presentation there is usually more discussion on the strengths/ areas for improvement.

Advantages are the greater freedom and flexibility in drawing up the initial data. There is extensive involvement by assessors with the unit in the site visit/evaluation stage. This is a very thorough process with high accuracy. Assessors obtain a multi-faceted viewpoint. The assessors are managers of standing in the organization and this gives a high degree of authority and credibility.

Disadvantages include the strong role of the assessor team, which places greater importance on their authority and credibility. There is a difficulty of getting the right people. A heavy involvement and commitment are required from the assessor team.

Workshops

DATA COLLECTION

The management team receives awareness training, plus some preliminary case study experience, on the model and scoring process. It then agrees allocation of responsibilities for collecting data among the team members. Alternatively, each team member may be asked to carry out a complete assessment of all nine criteria. Data is then collected by the management team members and they can use a variety of methods, from questionnaires, review of existing management information, or simply drawing from their own experience and knowledge.

POSITION REPORT

There is no formal position report.

MANAGEMENT AGREEMENT

There is no formal stage for management to endorse the data collected.

ASSESSMENT AND SCORING

The output of the data collection stage is recorded briefly by each team member on a pro forma showing the main sources of information, the strengths and areas for improvement, and the score for those criteria allocated to the team member.

CONSENSUS PROCESS

Each member of the management team presents evidence and recommendations for strengths/areas for improvement (in the case of allocated criteria), or the collected views of all team members are summarized (in the case of a complete evaluation by each member). This is followed by a consensus and scoring discussion. This also needs two facilitators who are also fully trained assessors.

SITE VISIT

There is no site visit. Any clarification needed can be arranged separately by the team members.

FEEDBACK REPORT

There is no formal feedback report. The output of the consensus meeting is a series of agreed pro formas, and a score. The management team which produced this output can then translate this immediately into an action plan.

Advantages include: management involvement exercise and ownership of the process; shortened time-scale for data collection; good educational value for management. The approach can lead straight into action planning.

Disadvantages include the less rigorous data collection than full assessment, therefore the approach is less accurate. There is the possibility of 'rose-coloured spectacles' by management. There is no objective, third-party inputs/validation/calibration. A lot of management commitment and time is required.

Matrix

MATRIX PREPARATION

In this approach the company 'customizes' its own framework for self-assessment around the nine criteria of the model. A series of steps or levels of achievement are drawn up, based on subcriteria and areas to address. A trained assessor team is required to draw up the matrix, and to select the relevant levels of achievement. The management team endorses the matrix and associated self-assessment processes. Some awareness training in the model for the management team members is necessary.

DATA COLLECTION

There is no formal data collection. Information is collected by a team based on the existing knowledge of its members. Membership therefore represents a cross-section of the unit being assessed. Alternatively the team can be the management team itself. A customized pro forma or questionnaire might also be used to derive information related to the achievement levels in the matrix.

POSITION REPORT

There is no position report.

MANAGEMENT AGREEMENT

There is no separate stage for management agreement.

ASSESSMENT AND SCORING

The rating is done against the matrix individually by team members based on their own knowledge of the unit concerned. All the team member is asked to do is to assign, by colour coding, the level of achievement on the matrix. There is no quantitative scoring. Assessors need awareness training in the model.

CONSENSUS PROCESS

The team meets for a consensus workshop, with the assistance of a facilitator, to agree a common rating. Because there is an assumption of pre-existing knowledge of the unit, there is less scope for using an outside organization to carry out the rating. It is essentially a unit looking at itself.

SITE VISIT

There is no site visit.

FEEDBACK REPORT

The output of the consensus meeting is an agreed rating against the matrix. There is no separate feedback report.

Advantages include customization to the organization's needs and a practical, quick and simple guide to attainment. Its ease of use may be motivational. It can be used at various levels of the organization. There are good opportunities for managers to be involved and to drive the self-assessment, closely linked to action planning.

Disadvantages include the limited selection of European Business Excellence Model subcriteria. The achievement of 'excellence' is over-simplified. There are possible distortions in management priorities; differing interpretations of the level requirement. The rating system is subjective. There is relatively low accuracy, and little opportunity for external benchmarking.

Questionnaire

QUESTIONNAIRE PREPARATION

The questionnaire is used to carry out a quick assessment of where an organization stands in relation to the model. It is most often used as a preliminary to starting one of the other approaches. The questionnaire can vary from a simple 'health check' to a sophisticated multiple choice questionnaire with scoring system and weightings. In the simpler versions, it can be used to test the self-assessment approach, or to interest the management team in finding out more. In the more complex versions, it can provide an alternative to the full self-assessment process.

DATA COLLECTION

The questionnaire is carefully drawn up to cover all aspects of the model, criteria, subcriteria and areas to address. It may be simply a tick list format, with multiple choice answers, from which a score can be derived, or it may have a more open structure with a built-in scoring process. It may be supported by 'write-in' comments or supplementary interviews. The questionnaire can be sent to a sample of employees, or to all employees in the unit being assessed.

POSITION REPORT

There is no formal position report. The results of the questionnaire returns, as summarized, constitute the data input for evaluation.

MANAGEMENT AGREEMENT

There is no separate management agreement stage.

ASSESSMENT AND SCORING

The output from the questionnaires is a multi-point perspective. The cumulative results can be regarded as the assessment, or can be used as the basis for a team evaluation by management or trained assessors. A pro forma approach can be used to summarize strength/areas for improvement, and a score can be assessed based on the summarized questionnaire results. This can be done individually by team members, or by the team as a whole.

CONSENSUS PROCESS

This is held when the team is using the questionnaire summary as a basis for an evaluation against the criteria and scoring of the model.

SITE VISIT

There is no site visit.

FEEDBACK REPORT

If there is a team assessment based on the questionnaire summary, a feedback report is issued, with the consensus score.

Advantages include the fact that this process can be structured closely to the model. It is relatively easy and quick to understand and use. It is also a useful introduction to the model, and a good method for getting widespread feedback from the people in the unit.

Disadvantages are that it is very dependent on the skill in drawing up the questionnaire, but always appears more prescriptive than the award-style self-assessment. It is never as thorough and accurate, nor as reliable a guide to action planning.

References

1. European Foundation For Quality Management. *Self-Assessment 1996 Guidelines*, EFQM, Brussels.
2. British Quality Foundation. *Self-Assessment 1996 Guidelines*, BQF, London.
3. European Foundation For Quality Management. *The European Quality Award 1996 Application Brochure*, EFQM, Brussels.
4. British Quality Foundation. *The 1996 UK Quality Award Application Brochure*, BQF, London.

4
Getting started

As we saw in Chapter 3, there are several ways in which organizations can tackle self-assessment. Whichever approach is adopted, the fundamentals of effective implementation are the same:

- senior management support and involvement
- a clear plan of action
- good people with the right skills and resources to make it happen
- everyone is aware of what is going on.

To facilitate the planning of self-assessment the EFQM has produced a flowchart of general steps involved in the overall process, as shown in Fig. 4.1.

This chapter looks at the first four steps of the overall self-assessment process, namely:

- developing commitment
- planning the self-assessment process
- establishing and educating teams
- communicating plans.

Developing commitment

Let us be clear. The success of self-assessment is very much dependent on the support and commitment of the chief executive and senior management team. Without their support it is unlikely that the people, time and resources needed for the self-assessment process will be made available. Also, they must own the product of the self-assessment; the information is an input to the business improvement process.

An important step on the road to gaining top management commitment is to ensure they have an appreciation of what is involved in the self-assessment process and to give them an overview of the European Business Excellence Model and how it can be used as a flowchart of business excellence. A one-day workshop with some hands-on experience of self-assessment using a short case study is a good way of achieving this step.

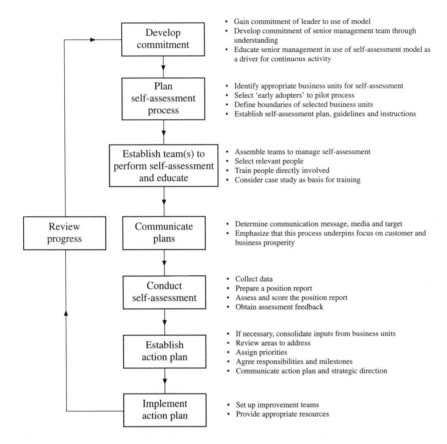

Figure 4.1   Self-assessment overall process flow (modified from EFQM source)

A typical one-day senior management workshop describes the European Business Excellence Model, the overall self-assessment process and the various methods of self-assessment. In our experience two short syndicate exercises on scoring and consensus featuring two extracts from an EFQM training study (e.g., leadership and customer satisfaction) help to enhance the participants' appreciation of the concepts. In addition – and this is important – careful consideration should be given to the reasons for doing self-assessment. Senior managers usually wish to debate some of the pros and cons.

Senior managers often prick up their ears at the mention of the word 'award'. They need to understand that the purpose of self-assessment against a model of excellence is not to enter a competition. In fact, very few, perhaps as few as 1 per cent, of the companies using self-assessment actually consider entering for an award. Senior managers need to understand that self-assessment is an internally applied diagnostic tool which provides the following:

- a rigorous and structured approach to business improvement
- an assessment based on facts and not individual perception
- a means to achieve consistency of direction and consensus on what needs to be done.

All managers should understand that self-assessment is a means to an end, not an end in itself. Understanding is enhanced if the reasons for doing self-assessment are posed in very simple terms. For example, self-assessment will help us to answer the following questions:

- How good are we really?
- What exactly are we doing to improve the business?
- How effective have our efforts been?
- What do these efforts have to do with each other and with our success?
- How do we get the most out of our efforts?
- How can we make sure our efforts are helping us to achieve our goals?
- What are we missing?

Self-assessment against the European Business Excellence Model will have a significant impact on your company – and that is an understatement. Setting-up and managing the self-assessment process is a major cross-functional project, the outcome of which will significantly impact the top team's agenda.

Therefore, it is vital that a senior manager acts as the project champion. The project champion should be a member of the board or the equivalent senior management team – in some companies, the chief executive undertakes the task. The project champion must have sufficient authority to help keep things moving and to overcome any major obstacles to progress.

Whether acting as project champion or not, the chief executive should stay closely involved with the process. It is no coincidence that past winners of the European Quality Award, and of the Malcolm Baldrige National Quality Award (see Chapter 14), highlight the active participation of the chief executive. Whereas, unsuccessful applicants (i.e., those applicants not receiving a site visit) often display insufficient senior management involvement, which is usually indicative of the company's approach to business excellence in general. Experienced assessors can usually tell if senior management commitment is only 'skin deep'.

Another way of involving senior managers is to encourage each of them to become a criterion champion. In some companies each criterion is 'owned' by a senior manager, whose responsibility it is to ensure that the data collection team gains access to all the relevant information and evidence relating to 'their' criterion.

Planning self-assessment

In planning a self-assessment programme the sponsors – the management team – need to consider a variety of issues concerned with people (e.g., team members, roles and responsibilities), processes (e.g., training and communication), information (e.g., sources and data collection), resources (financial, material and human) and the time-scale. The solutions are very much dependent on the organization's own particular set of circumstances. That said, in our experience, managers typically ask the following types of questions – many of which cover the award simulation approach:

Preparing for the assessment programme

• Which approach to self-assessment best suits our needs?

This depends on your available resources and on your purpose for undertaking self-assessment. Clearly, if your company intends to apply for an award then you will have no choice but to adopt the award simulation approach, although you should bear in mind that probably only 1 per cent of organizations undertaking self-assessment have any intention of applying for an award.

The scope and depth of information you expect from a self-assessment will condition your choice of approach, as will the speed of response. The questionnaire, matrix and workshop approaches yield a 'quick-and-bright' assessment, but do not provide the scope and depth of information that can be obtained from the award simulation or peer involvement approaches. Of course, the latter two are more time-consuming and resource hungry. To be done properly, an award simulation approach will probably take up to six months of effort, but the outcome will be a rich database of business excellence.

• A preliminary pilot or organization-wide roll out?

There is nothing to stop a company applying self-assessment across the whole organization from 'day one'. But this is a brave decision. Most organizations will seek to pilot the self-assessment programme on a relatively small scale in order to assimilate the practicalities of implementation. They recognize that they are unlikely to get it completely right first time and regard a pilot as a crucial learning opportunity. A pilot does not have to be limited to one area. It is possible to test more than one approach to self-assessment if more than one pilot area can be identified.

- Which business units should be assessed first?

To answer this question you need to ask others:
  - Which business unit management team is likely to be the most enthusiastic? And is it likely to succeed?
  - Can all the criteria of the European Business Excellence Model be applied to the unit in question? Who are the unit's customers? What are its key processes? What are its critical business results?

- How many assessor teams are required?

This depends on the number of business units you wish to assess as separate entities, or whether you intend to assess the company as a composite whole. You will need around six or seven people in each assessor team. If you intend to pilot in only one unit then only one assessor team is required initially. However, most companies, in our experience, tend initially to train up 20 people as assessors, thereby building an in-house resource.

- Whom do we need to train?

In addition to the assessors, all members of the data collection team(s) plus some senior managers – particularly those who will act as the project champions (see the next section 'Establishing and educating teams').

Data collection and presentation

- How do we collect the data?

Most companies use a variety of data collection methods such as questionnaires, check-lists, interviews, focus groups and so on. To produce a position report the company forms a data collection team and takes a structured approach combining some, if not all, of these techniques. It is worth while considering giving members of the data collection team at least a one-day appreciation of data collection methodology (see Chapter 5). A data collection plan will be needed.

- What are the likely sources of data?

A multi-disciplinary data collection team will know where to look; people will have ideas. One way is to consider drawing up a matrix of likely data sources within the organization. If a position report is to be prepared, then a structured approach is essential.

- How do we present the data for assessment?

The way the data is presented depends on the approach taken. If it is your intention to develop a business excellence database on the basis of self-assessment, and to use this database as a business improvement planning input, then you will need to write a position report.

The assessment

- Who is going to assess whom?

In some of the approaches the organization's own people make the assessment. In others, an external assessor is involved. Experience shows that an assessment is best done by the people not involved in assembling the data. The roles of data collection/presentation team member and assessor are best split. It is unrealistic to expect people to assess themselves objectively.

- Should we adhere to the scoring guidelines?

Think twice before changing a tried and tested model of excellence (such as the European Business Excellence Model). Some organizations do tailor the model to suit their own needs. They may, for example, change some of the scoring weightings of the model criteria. There is no reason why they should not. But they should avoid tinkering with the 50–50 split between enablers and results. Some organizations alter the terminology of the detailed areas to address to suit their own terminology but ensure the meaning remains unchanged.

One major advantage of leaving the scoring and weights unchanged is the ability to benchmark against other organizations who have used the unadulterated model.

- How is the assessment result fed back to the business unit?

In some cases the approach followed does not involve feedback from assessors; in others (e.g., award simulation, peer involvement, and sometimes questionnaire) there is a feedback report. We suggest that the person leading the assessor team (the senior assessor) be prepared both to make a verbal presentation of the findings and to discuss them (see Chapter 9).

Managing the programme

- Who steers the programme?

The senior management team, one of whom acts as project sponsor – facilitated by a good project manager. As the organization's use of self-assessment matures, the senior managers will become increasingly more active in the process as they see the benefits realized.

- What is the best way to manage the programme?

Experience shows that the self-assessment process, just like any other specific piece of work involving the activity of more than one person, has a much greater chance of success if the assignment is treated as a project.

Establish a simple project management structure with clear milestones for both activities and review meetings. The project team should meet for a couple of hours at least weekly. Avoid formally recording meeting minutes, as this is time-consuming and can 'bureaucratize' the process. Simple project review sheets, in the form of a matrix of actual performance against planned milestones, with space for explanatory comments of exceptional items, are usually sufficient for monitoring project performance.

In addition, the senior management team should meet with the project manager monthly to review progress. These meetings are an opportunity to build and sustain senior management ownership as the body of assessment evidence – the position report – is created.

- How often should we repeat the process?

Most organizations conducting self-assessment tend to follow an annual cycle. Done annually, self-assessment is a major input to the business planning cycle, providing an annual benchmark of progress.

Establishing and educating teams

For most of the self-assessment approaches outlined in Chapter 3 (peer involvement, workshop, matrix and questionnaire) the involvement of managers and other personnel is direct and clearly defined, and the educational requirements are straightforward (usually learning is a natural consequence of involvement). The people who receive most training are the assessors and facilitators, who are often external consultants.

However, the roles and training requirements for participants in an award simulation may be less clear. Therefore, this section concentrates on establishing and educating teams for an award simulation approach to self-assessment.

Team roles

Basically, three categories of team have a role to play:

1. the management team

2. the data collection team
3. the assessor team.

Members of the organization will contribute to each of the three teams, so you should be aware of the resource and educational implications.

The management team

Members of the senior management team can play an active role in the self-assessment programme by acting as project champion, criterion champions and assessors.

PROJECT CHAMPION

This is the senior manager responsible for overseeing the self-assessment process. In addition to acting as 'godfather', the project champion acts as the liaison with colleagues in the senior management team, and is usually the person who 'signs-off' the position report as a fair representation of the company/business unit.

CRITERION CHAMPION

This is a senior manager responsible for ownership of a criterion, thus ensuring that all relevant information regarding the particular criterion is available to the team preparing the position report.

The project champion and the criterion champions should, at the very least, attend a one-day awareness workshop along the lines described earlier. It is better still, if the project champion is prepared to attend a two- or three-day assessor training course. Certainly, all assessors must undergo assessor training if they are to be effective.

It is also a good idea to nominate a manager to become a European or UK Quality Award assessor or an assessor for a similar national/regional award. This will give someone in your company real-life experience of dealing with an actual award application as well as receiving assessor training. However, there are usually many more applications to become award assessors than places available. It is recommended that your organization nominates the most senior manager possible as general managers tend to get preference over quality professionals.

The data collection team

This is the group of people drawn from within the company or business unit charged with producing the body of evidence – the position report – for assessment. They are responsible for both collecting the data and writing the position report.

Experience shows that a 'workable' team size is five to nine people. While functional expertise is not essential for members of the data collection team, it is advisable to ensure that the team has a multi-functional composition. A broad understanding of the company's business and organization, both individually and collectively, is also important.

The data collection team is led by a project manager. The project manager is responsible for managing the complete project, including coordination of the input of the assessor team.

While the project manager does not necessarily have to be the editor of the position report, it is strongly recommended that the project manager undertakes this role, as it is pivotal to the whole process.

In addition to managing the self-assessment process to completion, the project manager does the following:

– oversees criteria interpretation
– assists in identifying sources of information
– edits the written sections
– ensures that the entire document is coherent and consistent.

Reporting directly to the project champion, the project manager should:

– be recognized as highly competent and credible
– have good interpersonal skills
– be a good communicator
– be reasonably numerate
– be a team player
– have a good knowledge of the organization's process network
– have a good rapport with other managers in the organization
– be self-secure.

Indeed, as with the other members of the data collection team, the project manager should not be a 'spare' who just happens to be available. If the exercise is to be a serious attempt at internal benchmarking, and if it is to be taken seriously within the company, then the people directly involved in preparing the position report should be among its best.

The assessor team

The assessors are the people responsible for reviewing and scoring the position report. In the interests of objectivity, the assessors should not be the same people who wrote the position report. This means that the assessor team should consist of people from outside the business unit being assessed. However, the inclusion of one person from the business unit may be considered permissable to help facilitate an exchange of ideas (although that person should not have been a member of the report-writing team).

The assessor team normally numbers six or seven people led by a senior assessor. The senior assessor's role is to coordinate the team's activities, ensure that the feedback report is written and communicate its findings back to the management team of the unit assessed. Ideally, the senior assessor is someone who has some assessment experience and, therefore, 'knows the ropes'. This is where a manager with external award assessment experience comes in useful. When starting self-assessment for the first time, some companies utilize the services of an experienced consultant or seek to borrow someone with assessor experience from another company, perhaps a customer or supplier.

Education

All members of the data collection and assessor teams should attend one of the EFQM or BQF approved assessor training courses. (The EFQM and the BQF licenses appropriate training organizations to deliver training courses based on EFQM's assessor training materials.) Alternatively, you can invite a licensed training provider to run a course for you in-house.

The purpose of such a training course is to enable those attending to gain a good understanding of the European Business Excellence Model criteria and of the assessment, scoring and consensus methodology.

The trainees practise the assessment methodology via a series of syndicate exercises. These syndicate exercises are specifically designed to enable trainees to do the following:

- Practise the art of self-assessment on a case study of a fictitious organization.
- Understand how to comment constructively on the strengths and areas for improvement of the assessed organization.
- Realize the issues involved in obtaining agreement to their views and judgement.
- Understand the practicalities of self-assessment.
- Begin to understand the logistical implications of implementing self-assessment.

All trainees receive an assignment some three to four weeks prior to the course. This assignment consists of approximately 15–25 hours of case study assessment. Completion of the assignment by all trainees must be considered as an essential prerequisite of attendance at the course.

Communicating within the organization

How much a company communicates about the self-assessment programme to its people will largely depend on its culture and management style. Some companies use self-assessment or an award application as an opportunity to relaunch their Total Quality or continuous improvement processes, using the momentum to give a renewed focus. Some companies limit their communication process to their own employees, others include their customers and suppliers.

The key points to be communicated include:

– the reasons for self-assessment
– the expected benefits
– who is involved and their roles
– the timetable for the self-assessment process
– what the European Business Excellence Model entails
– a basic appreciation of the assessment process
– what happens after the assessment has taken place.

Some practicalities

Based on our experience of working with various organizations, here is an outline of some of the practical issues which can arise during the implementation of a self-assessment programme.

Key players

● The key players are the project champion, project manager and senior assessor. All three must have seniority, credibility and sensitivity. Self-assessment requires exposing the darkest recesses of the organization to the light of objective analysis. Its key players must have the 'clout' to make things happen, the respect of their peers and the delicacy of feel to sustain confidence in the process.
● Trawl for potential candidates at the 'develop commitment' stage. Look out for the enthusiasts during the executive briefing sessions and appreciation workshops.

Programme implementation planning

● Organize the self-assessment programme as a proper project. Do not short-circuit project planning and formal review even for a pilot.
● Do not underestimate the time, effort and cost involved. A formal award simulation assessment can take up to six months, involve six or

seven people in a data collection and report-writing exercise, another six or seven assessors, not to mention overview by the senior management team. The cost? Compared to the information the process will generate, the money spent is likely to yield a significant return on the investment.

Pilot

- Select an appropriate business unit to pilot self-assessment before full-scale implementation. It may be appropriate to test out the pros and cons of different approaches to self-assessment by encouraging different business units to use different approaches. Another option is to pilot an award simulation by producing a position report on just a few (say two or three) of the nine criteria.
- Evaluate the chances of early success. Choose as a pilot the business unit most likely to make it work. Moreover, a volunteer will make a more persuasive advocate than a conscript.

Communication

- Be sure to make clear the benefits and the uses of the product of self-assessment. All too often management teams are unsure of what to do after the assessment has been completed.
- The business units undertaking self-assessment must understand the resource implications before they start. Incidentally, it is not advisable to start self-assessment at the same time as another major initiative – such as a new product launch, new software release or reorganization – the management team concerned will not give it their full attention.

Appointing teams

- It is often difficult to obtain the release of the best people to serve on the data collection or assessor teams. Getting them will be an indication of the commitment of their managers.
- Those companies that use self-assessment to best effect invariably perceive the process as an excellent people development opportunity. There is probably no other process that enables an individual to learn so much about an organization and its business so quickly.

Collecting data

- A systematic approach is essential. If a position report is to be produced then its quality is very much dependent on the effectiveness of the data collection exercise.

- It takes time. Allow sufficient time for collecting data; avoid the temptation to short-circuit the process. A comprehensive data collection exercise takes as long as, if not longer than, writing a position report.

Presenting data for assessment

- Understand the implications of the different approaches to self-assessment.
- Ultimately, a full position report is necessary if a comprehensive and in-depth study of the organization's current business excellence capability is required. The position report forms the basis for a 'live' business improvement database.

Senior management ownership

- In some of the self-assessment approaches (e.g., workshops, matrix) senior managers participate directly in the scoring process. However, where the assessment is based on documented evidence, such as a position report, it is important that the senior managers approve its contents before it is seen by the assessors.

  (The longer the document the less likely it is to be studied in depth by senior managers, so a thorough briefing of the senior management team by the project manager responsible for the report's contents is essential. Half-a-day should be allowed for such a briefing.)
- Senior managers should feel comfortable that the assessment documentation – the position report – reflects the 'way we do things around here'. Otherwise they are likely to feel uncomfortable with the findings of the assessor team as contained in the feedback report. Gaining senior management ownership is one of the most crucial elements of the process; without it the benefits of self-assessment will not be realized.

Conducting the assessment

- The assessment, whether it is 'internally' derived – namely, by a workshop or matrix – or 'externally' derived – through award simulation or peer involvement, must be professional and thorough. Even though the assessment is in-house the exercise should be accorded the same respect as a best practice benchmarking study of an external organization. After all, self-assessment is a form of benchmarking.
- Remember that the scoring is not a precise science. What is produced is

an assessment of the organization's current status not an accurate quantitative measurement of its performance, although the scores, when studied together with the EFQM's/BQF's scoring guidelines, do provide a useful benchmark.

Feeding back the assessment findings

- A detailed feedback of the assessor team's findings is essential. With the 'internally' derived approaches (e.g., workshop, matrix) the scores, strengths and areas for improvement are usually generated by the people who will be responsible for using the assessment findings. The feedback from an award simulation or peer involvement style assessment will take the form of a report. Care must be taken that it is constructive and 'reader-friendly'. The purpose of the feedback is to provide objective analysis and information, not to pass judgement. As the feedback is frequently regarded as judgemental, especially by management teams subjected to this kind of assessment for the first time, reports should be supplemented by appropriate verbal presentations and group discussions.
- Finally, the truth can hurt.

5
Data collection

The preparation of a position report is the sum of two equally important parts : data collection and report writing. The quality of the latter is very much dependent on the effectiveness of the former.

This chapter looks at what is involved in collecting the data from which the position report is produced.

Organizing data collection

Who collects the data?

The data collection team has a dual responsibility:

1. to collect the data and
2. to write the position report.

Experience shows that a workable team size is between five and nine people. The data collection exercise involves the collection team in several tasks:

- understanding the assessment criteria and guidelines
- creating a structured data collection methodology
- identifying who has the information needed
- interviewing people who possess the information needed
- organizing the data into a standard format from which to produce a position report.

Members of the data collection team do not need functional expertise, but a thorough understanding of the European Business Excellence Model is essential. This is best achieved through attendance at an EFQM/BQF licensed assessor training course – perhaps held in-house. A broad understanding of the company's business and organization both individually and collectively by the team is also important.

The nine key criteria should be allocated across the members of the team in such a way that each criterion has a member with a specific 'lead' responsibility. The lead team member need not be expert in the criterion, and there are some advantages in having a relatively non-expert viewpoint.

The role of team leader is important. In addition to taking part in the information gathering, the team leader's activities include the following:

– organizing the framework of visits and enquiries
– deploying the members of the team to best effect
– coordinating activities with management and staff
– compiling the data and editing the position report.

A possible division of the criteria among five team members might be as follows:

Member 1:   Leadership/Policy and strategy   (criteria 1/2)
Member 2:   People management/People satisfaction   (criteria 3/7)
Member 3:   Resources/Business results   (criteria 4/9)
Member 4:   Processes/Business results   (criteria 5/9)
Member 5:   Customer satisfaction/Impact on society   (criteria 6/8)

The precise allocations depend on the team size and competence. For example, a team member with an accountancy or a financial background might lead on (financial) resources and (financial) business results (parts of criteria 4 and 9), with another member taking the non-financial aspects of these criteria. Alternatively, for a company with strong engineering or technology competence, there may be a special need to consider technology applications (part of criterion 4) separately.

Whatever is decided on by the team, these allocations should not be exclusive. Lead responsibility means only that the team member concerned will take the main role in collecting data on that specific criterion. Other team members should be free to ask about or pursue issues on that criterion if the opportunity arises. Alternatively, the lead team member might ask another member to pursue specific questions during a particular visit or discussion. However, the role of the lead member on these occasions should be to collect the relevant data from other members, and to coordinate the input to the position report on that criterion.

Identifying information sources

Data gathering is a rigorous process, and must be done thoroughly if a meaningful assessment is to be made. The aim of data gathering must be to look at every aspect of the model, whether or not the data collection team thinks it is applicable to, or exists in, their own organization; and to find *how* things are done, and *what* have been the results in their organization.

Before going out and collecting the data, the team must look carefully at what information already exists in the organization, and will need to list the types and locations of the evidence sought. One way of doing this is to draw up a matrix to identify the primary sources of information for each area to address.

The data collection team should try to gather information from existing sources, not to open up new sources, or to create new classes of information. This may require some flexibility of interpretation from time to time, and some information may need to be presented in a form that had not existed before.

Remember that the objective is to take a snapshot of the organization as it is now, not how it thinks it is, or how it should be according to instructions, or how it plans to be. Above all, it must be a fair reflection of the organization.

The team leader, in discussion with the team, should prepare an activity schedule showing the allocation of criteria across the team, and the locations to be visited by the team members either together or separately. The production of an activity schedule will help in the following:

- to ensure that the data collection covers an appropriate cross-section of activities, people and locations to ensure valid results for the whole organization
- to avoid too many people going to the same site or discussing with the same people
- to plan the best use of team members' time and experience.

Developing a data collection questionnaire

The data collection team needs to develop a structured approach to its research by breaking down each area to address into statements and questions. Creating a check-list or questionnaire helps to put in place a systematic framework for gathering information before producing a position report.

The purpose of the questionnaire is to guide the data collection team on the right questions to be asked, and to suggest possible sources to check for the answers. The benefits of this approach are as follows:

- It supplements the team's training in the use of the model.
- It guides and shortens data gathering.
- It makes more efficient use of the team resource.
- It helps to tailor data collection to the particular company.

It also provides a standard methodology for ongoing and regular self-assessments.

Translating areas to address into questions makes it easier to communicate: asking someone a question is easier than explaining a statement; the more questions asked the more issues are uncovered and the better the questioner's understanding of the issues involved.

The data collection questionnaire covers all the relevant criterion parts of the European Business Excellence Model. The questionnaire is divided into two columns: 'questions to be asked' and 'evidence to be examined'. The questions column closely follows the model. The evidence column looks at the particular organization, and its scope and content are tailored accordingly.

To see how this works let us take a look at criterion part 1a: visible involvement in leading Total Quality. In the EFQM/BQF self-assessment guidelines the recommended areas to address for this criterion part include how managers take positive steps to achieve the following:

- communicate with staff
- make themselves accessible and listen to staff
- participate in quality improvement activities
- act as role models leading by example
- give and receive training
- demonstrate commitment to Total Quality.

An example of how the guidelines can be translated into specific questions and evidence prompts is shown in Fig. 5.1.

Criterion 1: Leadership

1a Visible involvement

Questions to be asked

i. How do managers communicate quality policy and other matters to their staff? What methods do they use? Do the methods meet the varied needs of the situation, and the staff concerned? Is there a consistency of style across the organization?

ii. How do managers make themselves accessible to their staff? Is there evidence of widespread 'open door' practices, and 'management-by-walking about'? Is there a positive listening culture adopted by management? Is this consistent across the company, and do all managers

Evidence to be examined

i. Take a sample of evidence from managers. List regular formal and informal methods of communication in use. Collect data on internal information distribution. Check relevant results of any internal staff satisfaction survey.

ii. Check any internal policy notes and/or training notes on 'open door'/'MBWA'. Examine physical limitations/opportunities for accessibility and free movement of staff/managers. Check evidence for staff suggestions/comments resulting in policy/process changes or other at all levels behave in this way? Are there any physical or other restrictions?

iii. How do managers participate in quality improvement activities? What kinds of participation do they adopt (initiating/supporting/team member/receiving and discussing reports/ deciding on recommendations, etc.)? Do they take part in team improvement activities beyond their immediate functional/specialist areas. Are top managers as involved as other managers? Is this participation a consistent feature or an occasional activity?

iv. How do managers behave as role models for quality in the company? Is there a clear perception that managers 'walk the talk'; behave according to the quality principles, including public accountability, published and known within the company; and how far do they lead by example? How clear is it that every manager is equally committed to quality? Does every manager equally demonstrate commitment to quality at all times? Is there the sense that quality has become the standard way they do things?

v. To what extent do all managers attend training in quality activities, and how far do they personally give and support training for staff?

vi. How far is visible involvement in quality a conscious, process-based activity by managers, and how do they review their performance? Does the company management team regularly review and improve its performance in these areas?

improvements in the Company. Check regular methods in use for upwards communication, records of regular outstation visits, etc. by top management, and any results from staff satisfaction surveys.

iii. Analyse numbers of improvement teams, projects, study groups, etc., spread of activities and representation by managers, and any internal statistics on time involved by managers on quality improvement teams' activities.

iv. Check evidence of management commitment from staff satisfaction survey. Search for examples of outstanding initiatives taken by managers, particularly top managers.

v. Check numbers of managers receiving quality training, and regularly giving training. Check range of training courses for managers, and those contributed to by managers.

vi. Check minutes/notes/records of management review meetings. Collect examples of initiatives taken to improve performance.

Figure 5.1 Data collection questionnaire – sample page

Collecting the data

Having developed an appropriate data collection strategy, and armed with a questionnaire or check-list, the team members are ready to start interviewing the subject experts. But before they do, there are some important considerations to bear in mind regarding questioning technique.

Using the questionnaire

The questions to be asked will affect all parts of the organization, and may involve all levels of personnel, so it is important that everyone involved in assisting the team understands the purpose and nature of the enquiries before the questioning begins. The data collection stage is a business improvement exercise in itself and must achieve the same standards of communication and effectiveness as any other business improvement activity.

The data collection questionnaire is not intended to be prescriptive down to the last piece of data. Judgement and flexibility are required. The important thing is to find out how things are done, not necessarily to get a precise answer to the specific form of the question (although this is the aim). If alternative information is offered instead, and it meets the spirit of the question, then its value should be considered by the team. But do not allow the questions to be tailored to the organization's environment to the point where they lose contact with the European Business Excellence Model.

Because it is based on a world-class standard of excellence many of the questions may have 'nil' or partial answers at the particular stage of evolution achieved by the organization in its excellence programme. This does not mean the questions are invalid. They are there to act as a standard for future achievement.

Do not use the questionnaire to critique the organization. It is a tool to help the team, and not a weapon with which to batter management! Also avoid the temptation to start taking any corrective actions or other related initiatives as result of information emerging during the data collection stage. This will dissipate effort and cut across the purpose of the exercise.

Where a question suggests some attempt at assessing the effectiveness of a particular process, its purpose is not to initiate a discussion on the strengths and weakness of the existing activity, but to search out any gaps between what should happen and what happens in practice. This makes site visits and on-the-spot enquiries particularly important.

The data collection process emphasizes the need for verifiable facts, not anecdotes or isolated events. If something happens only partially in the organization, try to assess the percentage achievement numerically, or qualitatively (high/most/some/little/none). This will help the subsequent evaluation process. The presentation of results data is also rigorous. Quantitative and statistically valid information is required, with trends over a period of years, and targets.

Interviewing subject experts

Interviewers must attempt to obtain the facts without being too intrusive. Anecdotal responses may well signify wishful thinking rather than reality. For example, a story about exceptional service, a testimonial from a delighted customer, or a promise to implement a better process next financial year are typical responses, especially by senior managers. But interviewers must politely ask for more:

- How do we do this?
- Where do we do this?
- How often do we do this?
- What is the process?
- How do we improve it?
- What are the results?
- How well are we doing against out own targets?
- How do we compare to our competitors?
- How do we compare to the world's best?

Furthermore, the interviewer must ask for data for graphs and charts that support what the expert is saying. You may not receive it straightaway, but now is the time to ask, not later.

When you request data be specific in the form in which you want the data. Tell people exactly what data you need, and ask them to keep copies of everything they give you. The copies will be a useful reference later, particularly if your organization incorporates a site visit into the self-assessment programme. In any case, one of the most important outcomes of self-assessment is the creation of a 'live' business excellence database to support a business performance improvement strategy.

Managing the data

The first part of this task actually begins during the interviews, by taking good notes and requesting documentation.

Upon receipt ensure that all data is word-processed, so that through your computer network it becomes accessible to all members of the team. This is invaluable for cross-referencing and for searching information on specific topics.

A good filing system is also invaluable. As data is collected either through interviews or documentation, it should be identified by criterion, by area to address and by source.

6
The position report

The position report is the body of evidence that describes your organization (or part of it) in terms of the criteria of the European Business Excellence Model. Having assembled and presented the information in the form of a single document, you will have probably created something unique. Almost certainly, no other document will have described the organization so comprehensively, in such a concise form and in a manner so potentially useful to the management team.

When preparing an application for, say, the European or UK Quality Award, an organization must produce a document that fulfils the requirements of a strictly enforced set of regulations. But for the purposes of self-assessment there is no one right way to produce a position report. You are not obliged to write a full award-style report of 75 pages – although many organizations do. Some organizations produce a summary-style report of perhaps no more than 20–25 pages; a few compile considerably more than 75 pages and incorporate the supporting evidence into the report. However, irrespective of length and format, the production of a position report is still a demanding and time-consuming task.

This chapter looks at what is involved in writing an award position report of around 75 pages.

Writing the first draft

Based on our experience of working with various organizations, here are some of the practicalities of writing the first draft of a position report:

Understanding the assessment criteria

Before writing, re-read the assessment guidelines to refresh your memory of the relevance of the section you are about to write. Be clear on what you are about to write and how it relates to the rest of the criterion both in approach and deployment (in the case of enablers) or in excellence of the results and scope (in the case of results).

Having enough data available

Once you understand the criteria, determine if you or other team members have gathered enough data to enable you to write an adequate response. Are you sure you really have all the information you need? If not, delay writing until you do. If necessary go back and dig deeper, it will be worth the effort; the richer your data the more factual will be your response.

Writing as a report

The accumulated data should be compiled into the form of a report; a commentary of your present position with regard to each criterion and criterion part.

Layout

At the beginning of the position report there should be a one- or two-page description of the company or business unit and, if part of a larger group, of how it fits into the big picture. This should outline the organization and the senior management's roles and responsibilities.

Each page of the position report should be numbered. This will help in cross-referencing and will greatly assist the assessors. Heading each page with the criterion number also helps.

A position report ideally should be no longer than that for an award application (i.e., 75 pages or less). In addition to assessing overall length, consider the length of each criterion part. It makes sense to allocate pages according to the value of the criteria. Table 6.1 shows an example.

Table 6.1 Page allocation

Criteria	Total points	Approx. no. of pages
1. Leadership	100	7
2. Policy and strategy	80	6
3. People management	90	7
4. Resources	90	7
5. Processes	140	10
6. Customer satisfaction	200	14
7. People satisfaction	90	7
8. Impact on society	60	4
9. Business results	150	10

One or two pages more or less per criterion, especially for the higher weighted criteria, will not matter, but significant disparities should be closely examined, for example, 20 pages devoted to leadership and only 10 devoted to customer satisfaction is probably not a good tactic.

Using graphics

Two well-known sayings, 'Every picture tells a story', and 'A picture is worth a thousand words', are particularly appropriate. As you write, you will discover places where a chart or graph will explain something better than words. When you do, sketch how the chart or graph should look or write down what you imagine and pass it to the subject expert and to the team leader.

This may seem obvious, but do remember to label and number all charts and graphs and refer to them in the text. Also, to optimize space, keep the size of charts and graphs as small as is practical, perhaps even down to one-quarter of a page.

Reporting on enablers   (How things are done)

A general point to remember when writing about any criterion or criterion part: it is vital to have before you the list of areas you are being asked to address. You must constantly read the guidelines as the document is being written.

Avoid anecdotal statements; the assessor is always looking for evidence. Anecdotal statements are not well received by assessors.

Do not neglect to state the position for the deployment as well as the approach involved. If the people doing the assessment have been trained well they will not assume that a good approach is used throughout the company unless it is stated, and supporting evidence is provided.

Keep in mind the salient parameters of approach and deployment. Approach is concerned with the methods the company uses to address the criterion parts. This will take account of the following:

- the appropriateness of the methods, tools and techniques used
- the degree to which the approach is systematic and prevention based
- the use of review cycles
- the implementation of improvements resulting from review cycles
- the degree to which the approach has been integrated into normal operations.

Deployment is concerned with the extent to which the approach has been implemented to its full potential. This implementation will take account of appropriate and effective application of the approach in the following ways:

- vertically through all relevant levels
- horizontally through all relevant areas and activities
- in all relevant processes
- to all relevant products and services.

Reporting on results   (What has been achieved)

You will need to provide multi-year trend data wherever possible. Where this is not possible, you must explain why. All key results must be compared with targets and plans.

One point to bear in mind: if the use of internal 'stretch' targets means that results consistently fall short of targets, you should explain the reasons why and provide supporting evidence.

Keep in mind the salient parameters of the excellence of results and the scope. The excellence of results will take account of the following:

- the existence of positive trends
- comparisons with own targets
- indications that negative trends are understood and addressed
- comparisons with external organizations including best-in-class organizations
- the company's ability to sustain its performance.

The scope of results will take account of:

- the extent to which the results cover all relevant areas of the company
- the extent to which a full range of results, relevant to the criterion, are presented
- the extent to which the relevance of the results presented is understood.

Noting and communicating criteria

As you write, you may also find your subject matter spilling over into other criteria and areas to address that are another writer's responsibility. You will, therefore, want to talk to the other writer to check that your text is not redundant or that the other writer is not missing an important piece of text.

Cross-referencing criteria

Cross-reference throughout the position report, where possible, to minimize repetition. Also, presentation of evidence elsewhere in the report may result in a clearer overall picture. For example, you may wish to show the effects of a training programme under customer satisfaction rather than people management. Where this is done, always remember to mention the cross-reference in both sections.

In any case, you will need to demonstrate the linkage between the enablers and the results for individual enablers.

Writing factual statements

If you make bold statements, be prepared to prove them. If you state, for example, that a process is a 'world-class approach' you had better have the evidence to support your claim. Assessors evaluate evidence not grandiose claims. Avoid anecdotes. The difference between an anecdote and an example is that the example illustrates the response, whereas the anecdote is the response.

Avoid generalities – e.g., 'all', 'every', 'very' – particularly if unsupported by factual evidence.

Writing positive, honest statements

This is sometimes difficult. There will be times when you think that your written response will not score as highly as you would like or believe is deserved. When that happens it is tempting to imply that you are doing more than you really are. Resist the temptation to deceive – the truth will eventually come out, and your credibility will be affected.

By all means demonstrate successes, but also include some situations and results that have shown up poorly and demonstrate what you are doing to improve them.

Writing in plain English

For the sake of clarity and completeness, always bear in mind that your eventual readers (the assessors) may know little about your company or business unit except what they read in the position report. Otherwise it is easy to assume a level of knowledge that does not exist, even if the reader belongs to your industry.

The key facts can also become obscured by jargon. You cannot completely escape your company's acronyms and jargon, but you can explain them in the text and in a glossary.

You may also wish to create a style sheet for uniformity. This should be done before the writing begins. The style sheet should inform everyone how to deal with specific style issues, for example: how to use variations of the company's names; how to refer to major processes; how to label charts and graphs; how to refer to other sections of the position report. Clarify these issues before writing begins, it can save a lot of confusion and correction later.

Make the report easily readable. The assessor wants an easy life.

Being selective

The assessor is always looking for evidence, so support your statements with examples and at all times demonstrate how you are measuring trends, etc. There will be many examples of development in your company so be selective – describe a few and demonstrate progress. You cannot cover all developments.

Evaluating the first draft

It is the project manager's responsibility to ensure that the first complete draft is compiled on time. When this has been done everyone involved in its preparation should meet to review the first draft. Such a meeting will inevitably take all day, therefore fatigue will dilute the effectiveness of the review process towards the end of the day. Two meetings of, say, 4–5 hours on consecutive days will be more effective.

The project manager should ensure that all participants receive a copy of the draft at least seven days before the meeting. All participants must be prepared to read the draft thoroughly, compare the responses to the criteria and come to the meeting ready to discuss it.

Typically, each criterion is reviewed by areas to address. Anyone can ask questions or make suggestions, with the comments directed to the person responsible for the criterion. The discussion should focus on interpretation of the criteria, relevance of the response and completeness of the response. Consensus is not always possible, so the final decision is best left to the editor. At this stage, the focus is on substantive issues rather than on grammar or spelling.

The comments of an outside expert will also prove valuable at this stage. An outsider provides an objective view. An insider will often be tempted to read between the lines of an assessment; an experienced external assessor will judge what is actually written. Also, the right expert will be able to share insights gained from experience with other organizations.

Producing the final draft

It will be necessary to write more than one draft. Before producing the final draft, print a few copies for proofreading and distribute them to team members and people who are good at proofreading. This eliminates the little errors which tarnish the quality of your document. Look out for misspellings, grammatical errors, misnamed or misnumbered charts, missing data or text and inconsistent references to titles, names and processes.

Finalizing the layout of graphics will take longer than you think. Allow as much time for their preparation as you possibly can. Have charts and graphs prepared as you write the first draft; do not postpone until a later date.

Charts and graphs should, as far as possible, appear on the same page as the text that refers to them, although this will become more difficult as the text is revised and charts and graphs are added or deleted.

One final point – and this applies just as much to a European/UK Quality Award application document as it does to an internal position report. A glossy, multi-coloured document is not necessary. A position report that resembles an annual shareholder report or sales catalogue does not add value to its contents. What is required is a clear professional-looking, well-structured and easy-to-read presentation. By the same token, black-and-white diagrams and tables are sufficient.

Monochrome text and graphics are much easier and cheaper to reproduce; an important factor if the position report is to be distributed widely. A simple comb or wire binding will also suffice.

7
Assessment scoring and consensus

While a position report is an extremely useful management tool, two further actions can maximize the value of what has been done. The first is to assess the organization on the strength of the evidence presented in the report by taking each criterion part and then computing the outcome to provide a 'score' out of 1000 points. This is the sobering part of self-assessment when some numerate answers begin to emerge to the questions 'Just how good are we?' and 'How well do we compare with others?' The second is to provide a constructive critique of what has been presented by way of a feedback report to the management team. This report highlights a number of 'strengths' identified by the assessors – those aspects of business operations that are to be admired. It also identifies a number of 'areas for improvement' – areas where significant gains could be made in the view of the assessors.

This chapter deals with the 'scoring' of a position report; Chapter 9 covers the feedback of the assessment.

The scoring system

Perhaps the most important observation to make right at the outset is that scoring of a position report is *not* a precise science. What is produced is an *assessment* of the organization, not an accurate measurement of its performance. Thus, the exact score achieved is largely irrelevant and, most certainly, to conclude that one company is better than another simply because it scored slightly higher in an identical assessment would be foolish. Having said that, scoring does give a good indication of where there is scope for improvement and it can reveal where centres of excellence exist within an organization. If you know where these are, the opportunities for learning through internal benchmarking are obvious.

The key document in the scoring process is the 'blue card' – so titled because of its colour! Its contents are reproduced in Figs 7.1 and 7.2. The card represents a set of guidelines to assist in assessing the capability of a company, for any criterion part, within one of four broad bandings. Thus, there are five defined points under both 'enabler' and 'results' headings, each expressed as a percentage. Clearly, assessors are not constrained to using just these defined figures; indeed, they are encouraged to interpolate between them to obtain a score that 'feels right' in the light of the evidence presented. However, the blue card acts as a valuable guide.

Let us look in more detail at the card and, in particular, at the key words that point to what assessors are looking for. Starting with Chart 1 (Fig. 7.1), enablers are the drivers of the business. They are the resources and capabilities that can be brought to bear to deliver some end result. Thus, the intention here is to investigate the approach adopted to ensure that enablers are being applied as effectively as possible, and to consider the degree to which the approach described is deployed throughout the business. Thus, the score arrived at for an enabler represents a combination of the scores awarded for excellence of approach and degree of deployment.

Usually, assessors simply take the arithmetic average of their two separate scores to give the final figure. However, there may be occasions when this is not appropriate. For example, a company may describe a superb approach worth 100 per cent, but reveal that it is not actually deployed anywhere. In such a case, the average score of 50 per cent would not make much sense! This illustrates an important principle of scoring which is that, having arrived at an average for either an enabler or a result, the assessor is encouraged to reflect on everything that has been presented and conclude whether the average figure 'feels right'. Usually it does, but not always.

Careful reading of Chart 1 reveals a number of key words that confirm what assessors are looking for. The key words are: evidence, systematic, prevention-based, reviews, integration and refinement.

Evidence: at all times, assessors are looking for clear statements describing what is in place and how things are done and offer data to confirm the extent of implementation. Thus, the following statement:

> XYZ company has a world-class employee training system in place and virtually all employees agree that it is the best they have ever experienced. The system makes sure that everyone has the skills necessary to do their jobs so that everyone contributes very effectively to meeting company goals.

is anecdotal and is not likely to impress an assessor. On the other hand:

> XYZ company completes a training needs analysis for employees as part of the annual appraisal round. The computerized system, known as TRAINER, matches job requirements against individual skills and identifies specific areas

CHART 1   The Enablers

The assessor scores each part of the enablers' criteria on the basis of the combination of two factors:

1. the degree of excellence of your approach
2. the degree of deployment of your approach

Approach	Score	Deployment
Anecdotal or non-value-adding.	0%	Little effective usage.
Some evidence of soundly based approaches and prevention-based systems. Subject to occasional review. Some areas of integration into normal operations.	25%	Applied to about one-quarter of the potential when considering all relevant areas and activities.
Evidence of soundly based systematic approaches and prevention-based systems. Subject to regular review with respect to business effectiveness. Integration into normal operations and planning well established.	50%	Applied to about half the potential when considering all relevant areas and activities.
Clear evidence of soundly based systematic approaches and prevention-based systems. Clear evidence of refinement and improved business effectiveness through review cycles. Good integration of approach into normal operations and planning.	75%	Applied to about three-quarters of the potential when considering all relevant areas and activities.
Clear evidence of soundly based systematic approach and prevention-based systems. Clear evidence of refinement and improved business effectiveness through review cycles. Approach has become totally integrated into normal working patterns. Could be used as a role model for other organizations.	100%	Applied to full potential in all relevant areas and activities.

For both 'approach' and 'deployment' the assessor may choose one of the five levels 0%, 25%, 50%, 75% or 100% as presented in the chart, or interpolate between these values.

Figure 7.1   Chart 1: Enablers
(*Source:* EFQM)

where employee development is needed during the coming 12 months. The system has been fully deployed through five of the company's seven divisions with complete deployment covering 100 per cent of employees planned for July 1996.

is much more likely to impress.

Accepting the need for evidence rather than anecdote, assessors are then concerned with ensuring that any approaches described embody the best principles of quality practice directed towards excellence, i.e., that they are:

- *systematic*: well thought through, competently applied and demonstrably fit for purpose rather than ad hoc
- *prevention-based*: geared to preventing failures rather than to detecting them after the event
- subject to regular *reviews*: with the emphasis on driving continuous improvement activity from data gathered on the limitations of current practice
- *integrated* into the mainstream operations and planning processes of the company rather than 'bolted on'
- the subject of deliberate and planned *refinement*: cycles driven by data gathered from reviews.

While these guiding principles provide a framework that encourages more consistent scoring, assessment is still subjective. For example, an assessor has to decide whether the information presented under any heading constitutes 'some evidence', 'evidence' or 'clear evidence'. However, knowing that this is the case gives an opportunity to those producing the assessment data to present information in the most favourable way. This is not 'cheating'; it is simply ensuring that you present the company as it is today honestly, but in the best light. Self-assessment documentation should seek to do nothing less.

Let us now turn to Chart 2 (Fig. 7.2) covering assessment of results. The intention here is to assess both the degree of excellence and the scope of your results. In presenting information for criteria 6 to 9, it is important that you help assessors understand just how good your results are. While the blue card gives several clues as to how this should be done, the most obvious requirement is not mentioned, that is, the need to ensure that any results presented are seen to be *appropriate*. That is to say, they relate to approaches which are being taken and presented under the enabler criteria.

Given that this is the case, the first thing that assessors look for is *trends*. That means presenting consistent measures of performance for some period of time and illustrating how they have changed. Improvement in a particular annual measure over one year will not be interpreted as a trend, although sustained improvement in quarterly measures over the same period will be

CHART 2   The Results

The assessor scores each part of the results criteria on the basis of the combination of two factors:
1. the degree of excellence of your results
2. the scope of your results

Results	Score	Scope
Anecdotal.	0%	Results address few relevant areas and activities.
Some results show positive trends. Some favourable comparisons with own targets.	25%	Results address some relevant areas and activities.
Some results show positive trends over at least three years. Favourable comparisons with own targets in many areas. Some comparisons with external organizations. Some results are caused by approach.	50%	Results address many relevant areas and activities.
Most results show strongly positive trends over at least three years. Favourable comparisons with own targets in many areas. Favourable comparisons with external organizations. Many results are caused by approach.	75%	Results address most relevant areas and activities.
Strongly positive trends in all areas over at least five years. Excellent comparisons with own targets and external organizations in most areas. 'Best in class' in many areas of activity. Results are clearly caused by approach. Positive indication that leading position will be maintained.	100%	Results address all relevant areas and facets of the organization.

For both 'results' and 'scope', the assessor may choose one of the five levels 0%, 25%, 50%, 75% or 100% as presented in the chart, or interpolate between these values.

Figure 7.2   Chart 2: Results
(*Source:* EFQM)

better received. On the other hand, a set of relevant and well thought out measures displaying a positive trend over three years will certainly begin to impress an assessor.

The second thing an assessor looks for is the use of *comparisons* that allow the company to assess its achievements relative to some benchmark. As a start, comparing achievements between different parts of the company can demonstrate an awareness of the importance of performance benchmarking. Much more impressive, however, will be the way in which the company uses comparisons with other organizations – ranging from competitors within the same industry, through to comparisons with acknowledged world leaders, regardless of industry. Being able to rank your company alongside others that have been selected for benchmark targets or are acknowledged as best in class or simply best will certainly justify higher scoring.

However, there is another vital aspect of assessing results. It is being able to confirm that the results that are being achieved by the company are due to the approaches described under criteria 1 to 5. Assessors look for evidence to confirm that good results arise from good practice, the approaches and extent of deployment, not purely from good fortune!

Finally, assessors look for evidence showing to what extent the results presented reflect the organization as a whole rather than just one or two parts of it. Most organizations can point to promising results in one or two areas. The truly excellent ones can demonstrate favourable results everywhere.

Once again, the scoring levels achieved will be subjective to some extent and little time should be wasted on agonizing over the last five or ten percentage points. We shall explore the reasons for scoring variation shortly, but one should bear in mind from the outset that assessment is not about precision. It is much more about providing valuable guidance.

Examples of criteria scores

A question that invariably crops up in company assessment is 'What would a really excellent score be?' The supplementary is always 'How far have we got to go to catch up with the best?' While repeating that the process provides an assessment, not a measurement, it is worth giving a general idea of what constitutes world-class excellence today.

There are several sources of data, the two principal ones being the score bandings achieved by the European Quality Award (EQA) – and prize-winning companies in 1992 and 1993 (bandings, because precise scores are not revealed). The second is the profile of scores given to each of the case studies by the many people who have attended the EQA assessor training courses. These case studies are readily available and provide a useful benchmark against which you can judge yourself.

However, a good deal of other information is also available – notably from the National Institute for Standards and Technology organization in the United States showing the profile of scores achieved by entrants for the Malcolm Baldrige National Quality Award since 1988. While not strictly comparable, this data confirms that the European and North American views of what constitutes excellence in terms of a score out of 1000 points is remarkably similar.

So what is the score for a truly excellent company? Allowing for variation in assessor markings, anything between 700 and 800 points represents genuine world class. Anything above 600 points represents a level of excellence to which few companies can aspire. A typical score for an organization that is being run competently and has a set of good results is 450 points.

But is a score of only 7 or 8 out of 10 for world class not a bit harsh? Only if we fall back into the trap of assuming that the EQA assessment offers a precisely calibrated measure. It does not. Assessment is always judged against a view of what constitutes excellence and that view will continue to evolve as time passes. Thus, an organization scoring 750 points today may work hard to improve, yet achieve a score of 750 again in two years' time. That does not mean that it has not improved. It means that it is still world class in the light of the increased expectations and perceptions of excellence.

Scoring variation

Why should there be any significant variation in assessing and scoring position reports when there is the blue card to guide assessors? In particular, how can extremes possibly occur? The answer lies in the fact that the objective and subjective assessment is done by human beings using personal judgement to assess, at face value, evidence presented in a written report. The only common factor shared by those assessors is that they should all have been thoroughly trained in the use of the EQA framework. Some will be industry experts, some technologists, some functional experts, some operational managers and so on. Each will bring a different perspective to the task of judging and each will view the written evidence in a different light. Does this variety present a problem? Possibly, in the sense that it requires a 'consensus-reaching' stage to be added to the scoring process, but this is far outweighed by the benefit of having the combined talents of a team of independent experts assessing your operation and providing you with comprehensive feedback on what they have found – both good and not so good.

Let us just look at what we regard as 'normal' and 'abnormal' variation. Normal variation is that which you would expect in a process like scoring, given its nature. The advice from those experienced in the art is that if a team of six assessors provide scores for any subcriteria which cover a range of 30 percentage points or less (e.g., scores ranging from 40 per cent to 65 per cent), then a satisfactory consensus score is achieved by simply taking the arithmetic average. Just to clarify the point, six individual scores of 40, 50, 53, 55, 60 and 65 give an average of approximately 54 per cent and that would be the conclusion of the assessor team. A combination of each assessor's strengths and areas for improvement are used to support the score.

Variation in the range 25–40 percentage points lies in the grey area between fair consensus and clear disagreement. The advice here is that the senior assessor should decide whether debate on the evidence is needed or whether arithmetic averaging will give a satisfactory result. Where scores are spread pretty evenly across the range, a likely cause is the personal value each assessor puts on the evidence offered. Averaging is probably justified in such cases. Where, say, four scores are bunched at one end of the range with two at the other, there may be a more substantial reason for the variation, such as key evidence spotted or missed. In such cases, debate is probably appropriate. In our experience debate usually ensues on each criterion part anyway, irrespective of the range of scores. The order of discussion on each criterion part can be decided in the light of the criterion weighting and score range.

Whenever variation greater than 40 percentage points occurs, then the probability is that there has been some misinterpretation of the written evidence. In such cases, the senior assessor would be wise to arrange for the assessor team to discuss the appropriate subcriteria scores with the aim of reaching a consensus view.

The consensus process

There are many ways of seeking consensus in a group when disagreement exists and there is, therefore, no 'correct' way. However, experience gained in assessor teams points to some useful guidelines for the person performing the senior assessor role:

1. Before the meeting, invite all assessors to re-read the report in its entirety to familiarize themselves with the evidence. Ask also that they review notes written in support of their judgement on scores awarded. Advise them of the subcriteria to be reviewed.
2. At the meeting, ask the group to re-read the evidence for each subcriterion under discussion (taking them one at a time). The aim is to review what is presented *in the light of what is being sought*. At this stage, do not reveal who has given what score. Then, ask for scores to be

exposed to the group. The purpose of this is to give any assessor the chance to change his or her score without any pressure from the peer group. In a proportion of cases, revised scores offered will be within a 30 per cent range and consensus may be deemed to have been reached.

3. Where unacceptable variation persists, open a short debate in which each assessor summarizes the significant points of the evidence presented in the position report that have determined the score awarded for a particular subcriterion. Do not limit the debate to the assessors with the highest and lowest scores only. That approach puts pressure on them to move towards the middle ground when they may have spotted evidence or omissions that others have missed.

4. Record the significant and agreed strengths, areas for improvement and site visit issues – preferably in a form visible to the group (a flipchart is ideal). This recording is important because the information will be summarized and used in the feedback report. Then, in the light of the information recorded on the charts, ask the team to rescore. In the vast majority of cases, acceptable consensus will emerge.

5. In rare cases where consensus still cannot be reached, the senior assessor should take a personal judgement of the view expressed and decide on a consensus score.

At the end of this process, the senior assessor will complete a consensus scorebook recording the agreed strengths, areas for improvement, site visit issues and scores on behalf of the group. This important document forms the basis for producing the feedback report described in Chapter 9.

The golden rules of scoring

In scoring a report, all assessors must continually remind themselves of a few 'golden rules'. The first and most important is that assessment must be based purely on the evidence presented. Furthermore, what is written in the report must be taken at face value. At all costs, avoid the temptation to think 'A likely story – I've tried that and it just doesn't work!' If the report says it works and presents evidence to back up the claim, then it works. Remember, the acid test on such occasions is 'Does it appear to work for them?' Any inconsistencies or doubts can be followed up at a site visit but, for the purposes of scoring, believe what is written.

The second rule is take into account only the evidence in the report. There is sometimes a natural temptation to feel warmly disposed towards an approach (particularly where it has served you well in the past) and assume that more has been achieved than is actually claimed. Beware!

Having issued the warnings, the third rule is not to be afraid of being out of line with other assessors. There are no 'right' or 'wrong' answers, only expert opinions, and yours is as valid as any other. Equally, do not become defensive in consensus meetings when others disagree. Listen to their views and allow them to influence you as you wish. Changing your position in the light of new understanding is a much-trodden and honourable path!

Finally, recognize that consensus means 'we are all pretty much of the same view now' – not 'we have finally got to the right score'. It cannot be said too often – the exact score is unimportant, it is what you do with the agreed views of strengths and areas for improvement that counts.

8
The site visit

During the consensus meeting issues will be identified which require clarification (i.e., to check or determine the correctness of evidence submitted). This may, in most cases, be achieved by reference to evidence that has been assembled to support the position report. In some cases, the assessors may wish to test such issues during discussions with the people who produced the position report and with others in the organization.

A site visit is an opportunity to talk with people in the organization and to enable the assessors to dig deeper and obtain a better understanding than may be possible from studying the position report.

Is a site visit necessary?

In the European and UK award schemes the site visit is an indispensable element crucial to the judgement process. The purpose of a site visit is to confirm the validity of an application for the award and to clarify any unclear aspects of it. The site visit also gives assessors the opportunity to 'put some flesh on the dry bones of the application', to get a feel of the company and to test whether it could be a role model for other organizations.

In the context of the award scheme, applicants are not allowed to bring forward any new information outside the scope of the contents of application document. The site visit focuses squarely on the application and seeks to substantiate the facts as presented. Based on experience to date, a site visit does not greatly affect the consensus score arrived at by an assessment team – perhaps by not more than plus or minus 10 per cent on the overall score.

However, the site visit is a flexible ingredient of the self-assessment process. If the purpose of self-assessment is simply to assess a position report and fix a benchmark for the organization then a site visit may not be necessary. Some site visit issues may be resolved simply by a telephone call or meeting, with, say, the project manager or other relevant people in the organization.

A site visit is a time-consuming exercise for both the organization undergoing the assessment and the assessor team. As it is a flexible part of self-assessment, why bother? Well, when planning your self-assessment process you might like to consider the two main benefits of a site visit:

- First, it will give you an enhanced external perspective if you allow assessors from another part of the company or from outside it to visit your site and interview your people. It also helps to orientate the assessors, deepening their insight into your organization and, therefore, ultimately adding to the quality of their feedback to you.
- Second, a site visit is an opportunity for your people to tell others what they do and how they do it. A site visit can have a positive effect on the workforce – and on the management team. It can act as a positive recognition of everyone's efforts.

If you decide to include a site visit in your self-assessment programme it is worth adopting the European/UK Quality Award site visit process and adapting it to suit your own particular requirements.

However, a site visit does not necessarily have to follow the guidelines laid down by EFQM/BQF as part of their formal award application process. A site visit can, for example, be integrated into the actual data collection and assessment process (see 'Peer involvement', pp. 35–36).

Planning a site visit

Preliminary planning of the site visit can and should begin at the consensus meeting. At that meeting the assessor team will have listed site visit issues with strengths and areas for improvement, and will be in a position to start thinking about the necessary arrangements.

Arrange dates

The first step is to fix the dates for the site visit. This is normally arranged through the project manager (the person within the organization who is responsible for coordinating the self-assessment exercise and for producing its position report), taking account of the wishes of the organization and assessor team.

A site visit planning meeting must be arranged with all assessors before the site visit. It is recommended that this takes place at least two weeks before the visit. This enables the senior assessor to advise the project manager of the assessor teams' requirements for the visit. For example, certain senior managers may be required.

The output of the planning meeting is a plan in terms of:

– which sites to be visited
– who will be involved (e.g., the whole team, part of the team, individuals)
– what information is needed
– how will questions be asked
– who will ask them.

Prepare list of items to discuss

In 1995 the European Business Excellence Model comprised 33 criterion parts and each criterion part can have a site visit issue. If at the consensus meeting, all site visit issues for each criterion part have been considered then there may be 70–100 site visit issues recorded. Clearly this quantity is too many to follow up on a site visit. It is therefore essential that the site visit issues must first be prioritized for each criterion. Furthermore, it should be recognized that some criterion parts have a greater weighting than others, e.g., customer satisfaction (20 per cent) and business results (15 per cent) versus impact on society (6 per cent). We recommend that in general there are no more than two or three site visit issues for each complete criterion.

When the list of issues has been agreed then the use of a site visit record book is recommended. The format of a typical page of a site visit record book is shown in Fig. 8.1.

Site visit record

Page 1

Application:
Site visited:
Senior:
Assessor:
Assessors:

Date:

1. Leadership (part 1a)

Site visit issues	Which site	Conclusions
	Who to see	
	Action by	

Figure 8.1 Site visit record – sample page
(*Source:* EFQM)

After the site visit and completion of each site visit issue a summary of the revised scoring results should appear in the final page shown in Fig. 8.2.

Site visit record

Final page

Criteria		Consensus score (%)	Adjusted score (%)	Weighting factor	Adjusted score (%)
1. Leadership	1a				
	1b				
	:				
	:				
2. Policy and strategy	2a				
	2b				
	:				
	:				

Figure 8.2 Site visit record – final page
(*Source:* EFQM)

Allocate items to assessor team members

There are several ways to allocate to assessors the task of checking the site visit issues. Some teams ask each assessor to verify all the site visit issues for all the criteria. This places a very large burden on each assessor and is not time effective.

We suggest allocating one or two specific criteria to each assessor and making them responsible to the team for the corresponding site visit issues. This method does not preclude other team members pursuing related issues and commenting on these to the assessor with overall responsibility for the criterion issues. It has a further advantage in that each assessor can be made responsible for completing specific sections of the feedback report.

It is worth noting that, in the case of an award application, in addition to site visit issues raised by the team of assessors the jurors too may make specific requests for certain issues to be verified or pursued.

Forward requirements to organization

The team will have identified the major areas of interest and should advise the organization in general terms. The team will have also identified key personnel in the organization who they think will be most able to supply the information.

For ease of communication, the on-site details should be organized by the senior assessor and the project manager. A short meeting between the two to finalize the arrangements may be beneficial.

During the site visit

If possible, it is recommended that the assessor team arranges a short introductory meeting at the beginning of the visit. During this meeting the senior assessor should:

- introduce the site visit team
- describe the process so far
- list the objectives and content of the visit
- allow members of the organization to introduce themselves and explain their functional responsibilities.

During the visit interviews with individuals and teams will take place. Private interviews should be permitted. There should be access to non-confidential minutes and access to any non-hazardous and other areas provided that such areas are not high security.

Remember, 'shop floor' employees will have been briefed and will expect to play a part. Try to ensure at least part of the visit involves some of these employees.

It is important that during the visit the team creates enough time for frequent team meetings to review progress. Arranging a dedicated team office is extremely useful. Do not be afraid to change your team plan in the event that new information becomes available. This information must be relevant to the position report and not additional information supplied after its preparation.

A short close-down meeting to make appropriate thanks to the organization's representatives and to say goodbye is recommended.

Above all, full confidentiality and anonymity should be uppermost in assessors' minds. Maybe it goes without saying, but assessors should conduct themselves in an impeccable non-reproachable manner.

The conduct of the assessor team is important during the site visit. The following European Quality Award Guidelines cover the conduct of the site visit team:

- Do not discuss with applicant
  - personal or team observations and findings
  - conclusions and decisions
  - detailed observations of the applicant's activities whether complimentary or critical

     – quality practice or activities of other applicants for the award
     – names of other award applicants.
- Do not accept gifts
- Do not leave with any of the applicant's materials.
- Do compliment for cooperation and assistance and, if appropriate, thoroughness of presentation.

You may adapt this code of conduct to suit your own organizational culture and self-assessment needs.

After the site visit

It is essential that a final team meeting is held immediately after the site visit. Site visit issues for all of the criteria must be discussed and agreed. A rescoring exercise is necessary using the same scoring/consensus process as used in the first assessment consensus process.

The framework of the feedback report should be agreed at the meeting.

It is the senior assessor's responsibility to coordinate the production of the feedback report. This does not mean that the senior assessor alone prepares the text. Specific criteria can be allocated to be written by individual assessors. The senior assessor then compiles and edits the complete report.

Keys to an effective site visit

Site visits can be tricky to organize and do well; the following list may assist you in maximizing their effectiveness:

- Ensure thorough and detailed preplanning by the assessor team.
- Have a clear site visit agenda.
- Define assessor assignments focusing on factors that have a significant effect on the overall score.
- Work as a team.
- Be prepared to adjust mid-course, but avoid surrendering the agenda to the applicant.
- Thoroughly document findings during the visit.
- Summarize findings immediately following the visit.

9
The feedback report

The feedback of an assessment is usually in the form of a report. The purpose of the feedback report is to give the organization being assessed information on the assessors' views of its strengths, areas for improvement and the scores.

The feedback is a crucial component of the self-assessment process. A well-planned and well-written feedback report acts as a catalyst for action, providing helpful and objective information to trigger relevant improvement initiatives. An ill-considered feedback report also acts as a catalyst – for inertia. A poorly written, badly constructed or unduly opinionated feedback report may well alienate the management team for whom it is intended, leading not only to arguments over content but also to possibly discrediting the self-assessment process itself.

In this chapter we shall look at the format of a feedback report and what is involved in writing one. But first let us quickly examine the inputs to a feedback report.

Inputs to a feedback report

Figure 9.1 shows the inputs from which the feedback report is developed. Each assessor independently reviews the submission document, completing a scorebook consisting of at least 1 page for each of the 33 criterion parts of the enablers and results. This exercise typically takes between 15 and 25 hours per assessor.

The senior assessor then arranges an assessor team meeting to review individual findings. This meeting, which can last a day and a half, is tasked with producing the content of a consensus scorebook/report in the form of strengths, areas for improvement, site visit issues and a team score for each criterion and criterion part.

The consensus report, which follows the same format as the original scorebooks, is a crucial document; it provides a check-list for planning a site visit (if required), and it is the basis of the feedback report to the assessed organization.

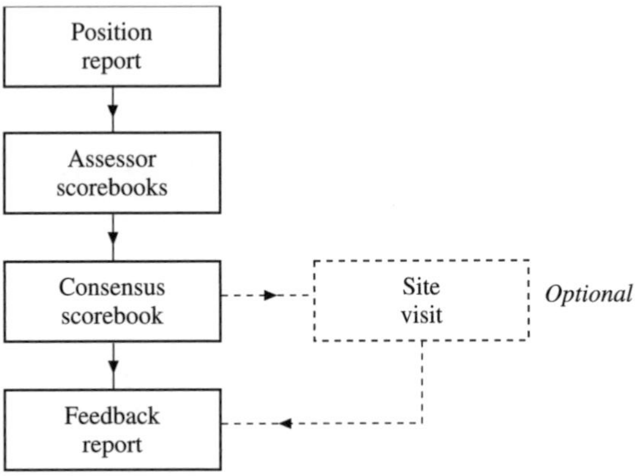

Figure 9.1   Inputs to a feedback report

Writing the feedback report

The feedback report has a basic structure to facilitate easy preparation of the contents. A feedback report could contain the following:

- a description of the assessment process followed
- a brief (say, one page) general impression of the position report
- for each criterion part, a list of
  - strengths
  - areas for improvement
  - a percentage score
- a scoring summary of the points scored overall.

The feedback report is produced by the assessor team. This can be done in one of two ways:

1. The senior assessor writes the whole report and circulates it to the rest of the assessor team for comment/improvement.
2. The senior assessor allocates team members to deal with a specific criterion. The senior assessor then brings together the complete report and circulates it to the whole team for comment/improvement.

The consensus scorebook provides the basis for the feedback report. This means that when producing the consensus scorebook the assessor team should give due consideration to the readability of their recorded comments. For example, shorthand phrases or even one-word comments should be avoided, because they may appear meaningless even just a few days later.

Furthermore, the feedback report should not recommend solutions. A feedback report should keep to the facts of the assessment. Comments should be restricted to what is and is not contained in the position report. The feedback is not intended to be a consultancy report. However, while involved in a self-assessment, if anyone has an idea for improvement it is worth while recording it separately for consideration at a later time.

Here are some hints on preparing a feedback report:

- Be tactful and constructive.
- Address key issues, focusing on strengths and areas for improvement.
- Use the words of the position report – avoid being a consultant.
- Be consistent with your scores. (High scoring criteria have typically several strengths and few areas for improvement and vice versa.)
- Make concise points and use short sentences.
- If possible, confine comment to areas directly related to the position report and model criteria and the blue card (i.e., the scoring guidelines).
- It must be understandable by the team responsible for the organization as portrayed in the position report.

The choice of the words used is important. Figure 9.2 is an example of an assessor team's comments on criterion 1a as contained in a consensus scorebook.

Figure 9.3 shows how the same list of strengths and areas for improvement could be written in a feedback report. Note the differences are in the main relatively slight, but the subtle changes to sentence construction do ensure readability of the recorded comments. The point is that a feedback report should be reader-friendly, after all, its sole purpose is to provide its readers (i.e., the members of the company or business unit that has undergone an assessment) with a usable guide for planning subsequent improvement activities. It is not an audit record.

The feedback report can be adapted to the needs of the organization. A document prepared for internal purposes does not have to be as 'judicial' as a formal award feedback report (e.g., from the EFQM or BQF). For example, it might go into more specific detail, perhaps giving a commentary of the assessors' overall perceptions of the organization's achievements against each criteria. It might reveal information on the scores and some comparisons with external benchmarks.

Moreover – in spite of our earlier comments – the report could be written as a consultancy report to the extent of including recommendations for further action. Some organizations prefer the assessment findings to be supplemented with constructive guidance notes and comments, especially if they are undertaking self-assessment for the first time. However, it is vital that the feedback report's basic award-style structure is not lost and it

---

CONSENSUS REPORT

1.   Leadership   The behaviour of all managers in driving the company towards Total Quality

- -

1a   How the executive team and all other managers inspire and drive Total Quality as the company's fundamental process for continuous improvement. Evidence is needed of visible involvement in leading Total Quality.

- -

Strengths

- Senior managers visibly involved in the TQM programme
  Steering committee has site managers and all directors as members
- Action steering groups are chaired by members of the senior management team
- Own managers used as trainers in rolling out TQM and more than half of the senior management team trained as auditors or facilitators and the managing director personally concluded 11 of 12 courses
- QA systems overseen by the steering committee
- Many channels of communication used by management
- Managing director has an approach of MBWA and spends ½ day per fortnight at each site talking to supervisors and operators

Areas for improvement

- Only recently started a TQM drive ... little evidence of refinement/review or durability
- Statements of MBWA and 'easy access' to managers tend to the anecdotal
- Not clear whether communication channels are used to communicate TQM issues (with exception of Quality News-sheet and anecdotal evidence in company newsletter)
- Nothing on involvement of lower levels of managers or supervisors except through team briefings

Percentage score	
Approach	40
Development	50
Overall	40

Figure 9.2   Consensus report – sample page
(*Source:* EFQM)

FEEDBACK REPORT

---

1.   Leadership   **The behaviour of all managers in driving the company
                          towards Total Quality**

- -

1a   How the executive team and all other managers inspire and drive Total
     Quality as the company's fundamental process for continuous improve-
     ment. Evidence is needed of visible involvement in leading Total Quality.

- -

Strengths

- The senior managers are visibly involved in the company TQM
  programme. The site managers and all the directors are members of the
  steering committee. The action steering groups are chaired by the members
  of the senior management team
- The company's managers are trainers in the roll-out of the TQM
  programme, more than half of the senior management team have been
  trained as auditors or facilitators and the managing director has personally
  concluded 11 of 12 courses
- The QA system is overseen by the steering committee
- Many channels of communication are used by management
- The managing director has an approach of MBWA and spends ½ day per
  fortnight at each site talking to supervisors and operators

Areas for improvement

- The company has only recently started a TQM drive and there is little
  evidence of refinement/review or durability
- The statements on MBWA and 'easy access' to managers tend to the
  anecdotal
- It is not clear whether the communication channels are used to
  communicate TQM issues (with exception of the Quality News-sheet and
  anecdotal evidence in the company newsletter)
- There is little evidence of involvement of lower levels of managers or
  supervisors except through the team briefings

Figure 9.3   Feedback report – sample page
(*Source*: EFQM)

becomes a discussion document, thereby losing its objectivity and undermining its credibility.

Finally, a presentation of the feedback report's contents by the senior
assessor to the senior management team is quite usual – and is
recommended. This is an opportunity to enhance understanding and to

gain senior management 'buy-in'. The presentation should take place around two to three weeks after the feedback report has been submitted to the senior managers, to allow everyone sufficient time to read and digest its contents.

10

The links to the bottom line

We all know instinctively that improving quality has to be good for our business. But why should shareholders be interested in, or believe in, our instincts? Why should the board continue to invest time and effort in something that does not have clear links to the all-important cash flow and profitability? Why should our employees squeeze an extra 1 per cent improvement when they have already worked what they believe are miracles?

Of course, there is plenty of evidence that big money can be saved through business excellence, particularly in the early days of an initiative when dramatic improvements in waste, re-work and productivity are common. But as progress is made and each successive improvement becomes harder, commitment can easily begin to wane. It is at this point a sad lament is often heard: 'If only we could be sure that our improvement efforts were meaningful. If only we could conclusively show the board that our improvement efforts really are linked to the needs of the business.'

Business excellence can improve business results. Indeed, we would go so far as to say that the prime reason for implementing business excellence is to improve business results through committed customers, as demonstrated by the European TQM model. Unfortunately, the links between business excellence and business results remain unclear in many boardrooms.

The problem for most business organizations is that management decision-making tends to have a short-term focus. Furthermore, management decisions are often taken in isolation without a clear frame of reference. On the one hand, operations managers often appear not to know how their decisions impact on business success; on the other, top managers seem uncertain how the various operational initiatives fit together to create value. The challenge is to understand what drives business success and to link operational decision-making to these drivers.

Created value

In Chapter 1 we stated that the creation of value is the basis of business, and that to achieve it all businesses use two main resources: intellectual capital (people's skill, time, effort and know-how) and financial capital (fixed or working). Intellectual capital is expandable through training and development. Financial capital is borrowed from investors or lenders, or is obtained by earning money from customers and retaining it in the business.

Why not then focus the key decision-making processes within the business squarely on the basis of created value? After all, the basic concept of creating value and using it for measuring business performance has been around since 1790. It has been the basis for measuring national economies since 1960 and is, therefore, well tried and tested.

At this point it is worth repeating the basic concept of created value and how this relates to the business excellence criteria. Remember that created value is based on a simple concept: sales revenue equates to the income from goods and services that have perceived value and benefits for customers. From sales revenue the expenditure costs of bought-in materials, supplies and services that have a perceived value to the buyer are deducted. The difference between sales revenue and expenditure costs represents the created value to pay for the cost of intellectual capital and financial capital (see Fig. 10.1). Only when all the costs of materials, supplies and services, intellectual capital and financial capital have been met has any real additional value been created by the company.

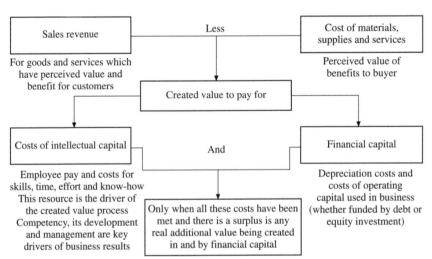

Figure 10.1   The created value concept

The financial performance of a company can be readily calculated using this created value concept. Created value is based on two foundations:

- the satisfaction and perception of customers and buyers
- the efficient combination of the resources of intellectual capital and use of financial capital.

Created value performance can be measured by three fundamental ratios:

- created value as a percentage of sales
- created value per unit of pay
- created value per unit of assets.

The created value concept closely follows and relates to the following six criteria of the European Business Excellence Model:

– Sales revenue	Customer satisfaction
– Cost of materials,	Process management
suppliers and services	Resource management
– Cost of intellectual capital	People management
	People satisfaction
– Financial capital	Resource management
	Business results

The relationship is shown in Fig. 10.2.

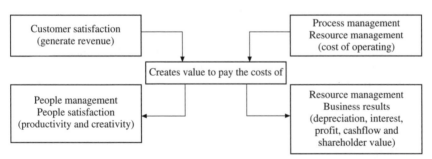

Figure 10.2   How created value relates to the European Business Excellence Model (1)

Figure 10.3 shows the relationship when we add the other three criteria of the European Business Excellence Model. So what started out as a *financial* model has now become an *excellence* model. By overlaying the two, we can see how the criteria of the excellence model relate to the key drivers of financial performance.

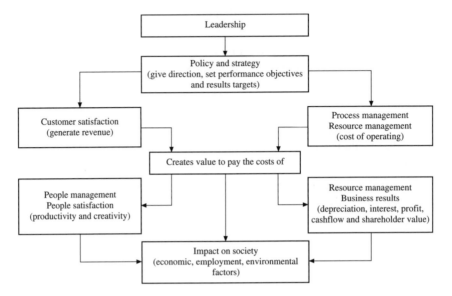

Figure 10.3   How created value relates to the European Business Excellence Model (2)

What drives business success?

The prime factors of business success are clear. They have been well studied and researched for many purposes, such as performance analysis, investment assessment and credit scoring, and are well defined in the following financial terms.

- sales levels, growth and continuity
- profit margins
- return on invested capital (i.e., net debt plus equity, relative to the cost of capital)
- cashflow.

These have all been linked to financial reporting, budgeting and monitoring systems. What is really needed is for them to be related to management decisions and the related measurement process. The European Business Excellence Model provides a sound and robust framework for this purpose. What many companies appear to be searching for is a framework for linking business excellence to a financial success model. Companies now seem to have accepted that it is excellence factors which are the prime drivers of business results – to which, in many cases, company directors' and managers' pay is linked.

Table 10.1 shows the prime financial success criteria and main success drivers. The European Business Excellence Model criteria can be rearranged alongside the performance measures and drivers as shown. This table indicates the structural links between the business success model and the business excellence model. Understanding this structural approach will show how excellence criteria can be linked to success factors.

Table 10.1 Business success links to business excellence factors

Primary measures of business success	Primary success drivers	Excellence model criteria
	The overall success of any business ultimately will depend on	Leadership Strategy and policy
Sales levels	Market sector activity, share, future development	Customer satisfaction
Sales growth	Innovation in products and marketing	
Sales continuity	Technological, process and competitive change	
Profit margins (all of these are part of being a low-cost operator and reflect the efficient use of resources)	Percentage of created value from each unit of sales	Process management
	Created value per unit of pay	People management People satisfaction
	Created value per unit of assets	Resource management
Return on invested capital

Cashflow | This reflects the generation of profits and the effective management of assets and cash which impact on shareholder value | Business results Impact on society Society in terms of funding of assets, employment levels and environment |

It is, therefore, possible for any company or business unit to accurately measure, track and benchmark the base drivers of business success using the following seven value performance ratios:

- sales levels, growth and continuity
- profit as a percentage of sales
- created value as a percentage of sales
- created value per unit of pay
- created value per unit of assets
- return on invested capital
- cashflow

Each of these value performance ratios relates to and is impacted by the criteria of the European Business Excellence Model as shown in Fig. 10.4.

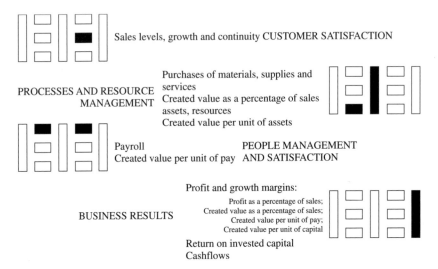

Figure 10.4   Value performance ratios

Focused decision-making

A created value approach allows a business to focus on the decisions that will drive business success and not just the results reported. It requires managers to think like investors and consider the long-term consequences of their decisions and actions. It allows top managers to see the tremendous impact that small changes in key decisions can have on created value, and enables everyone to understand how they can personally contribute to created value.

The outcome is a powerful mechanism for making business initiatives more effective. One that links boardroom performance to operating performance, and provides a way of bringing together directors, operations managers and accountants to focus on the business excellence factors that impact on business success.

Business success is dependent on managers consistently making the right decisions in four key areas: getting money in, controlling costs, the effective use of people and the efficient use of financial assets (see Fig. 10.5).

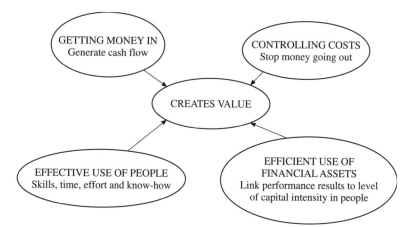

Figure 10.5 Making the right decisions

Each of these four key business success areas is linked to corresponding business operational issues as shown in Table 10.2. You can see how the various operational decisions combine to impact on business success.

How the four key business success areas impact on profit becomes even more apparent when Fig. 10.6 is considered. The profit increase percentage figures shown are based on the VI Group's analysis of the created value potential of over 630 companies in the FT non-financial index.

Table 10.2   How operational decisions relate to key success areas

Key success areas	Operational decisions
Getting money in (Generate cash flow)	Impact on price and volume positively or adversely Impact on customer satisfaction issues
Controlling costs (Stop money going out)	Influence any or all cost, use and waste of materials, supplies and services
Effective use of people (Skills, time, effort and know-how)	Ensure that adequate skills and abilities exist to operate the creating value processes and procedures effectively Eliminate the waste of all human effort and time
Efficient use of financial assets (Link performance results to level of capital intensity in people)	Develop the effective and efficient use of all equipment and working capital Reduce to a minimum any activity that prevents equipment from not being used to the maximum to create value Reduce to an optimum process throughput times

The potential impact on profits of making the right operational decisions highlights the importance of paying detailed attention to improve the sensitivity of all managerial decision-making.

Self-assessment against the European Business Excellence Criteria provides a potentially sharper focus on the decision sensitivities of the largely non-financial factors that really drive business results.

The cumulative effect on profit of small (1 per cent) improvements resulting from effective managerial decision-making can be phenomenal. There are seven key management decision factors (what we call the 1 per cent sensitivity factors):

- Prices   ↑ 1%
- Volume of business   ↑ 1%
- Cost of materials   ↓ 1%
- Use of materials   ↓ 1%
- Cost of expenses   ↓ 1%
- Payroll costs   ↓ 1%
- People effectiveness   ↑ 1%

Our research of UK listed companies shows that if all these factors had been

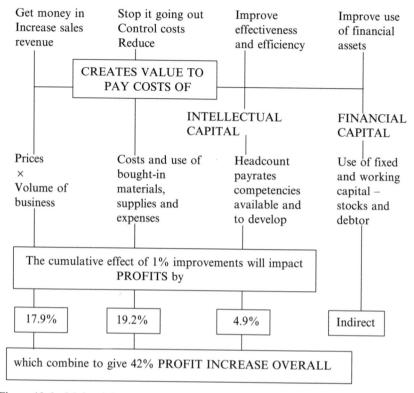

Figure 10.6   Maintaining or improving business results

altered beneficially by 1 per cent, then the impact on profit (based on 1992–93 figures) would have been to raise the profits as follows:

– for FT 100 index companies, by an average of 34 per cent
– for FT non-financial index companies, by an average of 42 per cent.

The effect of levels of improvement such as these on shareholder value would have been £270 billion on the FT non-financial company portfolio in the United Kingdom, as at the beginning of 1994. Even allowing for error in the sensitivity forecasts, the potential financial benefits from developing business improvement initiatives are significant.

Shareholder value

Is there a link between business excellence and shareholder value? Our research indicates there is a strong link.

Shareholder value is the sum of share price appreciation plus dividends over a period of time. Not surprisingly, it is driven by the same combination of factors which drive business success, namely:

- sales levels, growth and continuity
- profit margins
- return on invested capital
- cashflow.

Shareholder return is the sum of the dividends plus the increase in share price relative to the acquisition price of the share.

During 1994–95, Paragon Consulting Associates researched the links between business excellence and shareholder value. Studies of the existing independently selected top 20 lists of the Most Admired Companies and of 50 companies which were nominated for the British Quality of Management Award show that 21 of them are in both lists and were also among the 46 UK companies which were in the top 100 performing companies in Europe. Some of these 21 companies were also in several other international ranking lists.

An investment portfolio of these 21 companies was created and compared with the general investment performance of the 630+ FT non-financial index companies (see Table 10.3). This portfolio outperformed the FT non-financial index on many indicators, including:

- 50 per cent higher return on invested capital
- 44 per cent higher ratio of market value to invested capital
- significantly higher values for created value and profit as a percentage of sales.

Table 10.3   Paragon financial performance benchmarking study

	Portfolio	FT index
Percentage change over 3 years in		
Sales	23.0	14.4
Profits	5.1	−8.05
Created value	18.9	11.1
Payroll	25.4	14.8
Headcount	−5.1	−7.2
Performance ratios		
Percentage return on invested capital	18.3	12.82
Profit as a percentage of sales	11.33	7.45
Created value as a percentage of sales	34.75	30.26
per unit of pay	2.04	1.69
per unit of total assets	0.33	0.31
per unit of invested capital	0.75	0.68

This study shows that companies recognized as having excellence, quality and strong management characteristics are also very successful in traditional financial performance terms.

Another interesting point is that these 21 companies created over 58 per cent of the economic value generated by the whole of the 630+ FT index companies. These 21 companies represent 27 per cent of the sales turnover, use 29 per of the invested capital and 22 per cent of the employees to generate 30 per cent of the operating profits less tax and 26 per cent of the operating cash of the FT index companies. Economic value is calculated by making a deduction from operating profits less tax for the cost of debt plus equity. This cost of capital is calculated by the no-risk bond rate, inflation and a risk factor on equity. Only if operating profit less tax exceeds the cost of capital has any new and real economic value been created.

The top 25 per cent performing companies in the FT non-financial index needed (in August 1995) to continue to earn rates of return on net debt plus equity of over 20.2 per cent to maintain existing high performance. This is over 50 per cent above the median level of the FT non-financial index. Yet 26 per cent of the companies are earning less than the cost of capital: their shareholders would do better by investing in government bonds; their directors would do well to invest in developing a strategy for business excellence.

Investing in excellence

There are three key issues that all boards must address:

1. What will be considered as acceptable performance by the stakeholders?
2. How do we put together a balanced business strategy and structure to deliver the desired results?
3. How do we organize the resources to produce the desired result?

The approach to resolving these issues will vary from company to company.

Many large companies are, in effect, investment companies with funds invested in several businesses. For such companies the creation of shareholder value is based on their ability to develop an investment strategy and acceptable performance goals, and then to select the appropriate business investment opportunities – which may be existing subsidiaries or new ventures. These companies need to achieve synergy with existing investments and be in growth markets where they have some expertise. They need to do the following: set goals and performance benchmarks for acceptable business results; select and develop operating managers to run the business units; and create an acceptable business strategy and policy for managing the 'investment'. The European Business

Excellence Model provides a structure for managing an 'investment company' and provides a framework for assessing the quality of management in each business.

In small and medium-sized companies the functions of setting business goals, developing business strategies and plans, monitoring progress and operating the business are usually carried out by the same management team. This requires broader levels of expertise and experience in managers. The European Business Excellence Model provides a framework for developing a total management approach to delivering results.

In the case of publicly quoted companies another group of people are involved – the 'City' – the analysts, the merchant bankers, the institutional investors, the individual investors, etc. The major influence on the City here is their perception of a company's performance and results relative to alternative investments. The investors have an inherent need for their portfolios not to underperform certain sector and overall share indices in terms of growth of dividends and share price changes. The judgements involved are complex but mainly are about sales growth and managerial efficiency to maintain or improve margins and cashflow. The City makes judgements about the cost of capital (e.g., no-risk bond rates, interest rates, the risk factors and inflation) in order to determine the discount cashflow rate to use when calculating the share price. Since we already know the 1 per cent changes in key management decisions can increase profits by between 20 and 60 per cent then the City is in reality applying the same judgement criteria as contained in the European Business Excellence Model, although most investment analysts would probably not realize it.

11

Using the European Business Excellence Model as a strategic planning guide

The formulation of a company's policy and strategy is essentially an ongoing process of defining, prioritizing, organizing, achieving and reviewing world-class targets of business performance. To do this, management teams must focus on those areas critical to success by listening to the company's main stakeholders and identifying the performance levels that affect their satisfaction.

As we stated in Chapter 1, excellent companies do two things:

1. They focus on creating value above all else.
2. They make the right decisions to create value.

To such companies, value-based management is seen as a single focus shared by all. It is an approach that encourages all managers to think in boardroom terms like investors. They are forced to consider the long-term consequences of their decisions and to focus on continuing to deliver value to their customers, to their employees, to their shareholders and to society.

Excellent companies perform well in terms of sales growth, profit margins, return on invested capital and cashflow but are not obsessed solely with financial measures. They are equally obsessed with the apparently less tangible measures of customer satisfaction, people satisfaction and impact on society, recognizing that these are increasingly the real drivers of corporate success over the middle to long term.

In other words, excellent companies are concerned with aiming the arrowheads of their decision-making at the right value creation targets. The results criteria of the European Business Excellence Model provide a simple but powerful template for establishing relevant focal targets.

When we first used the illustration in Fig. 11.1, at public presentations, we jokingly suggested that TARGETS is an acronym for Take Aim, and Remember Get Everything Together ... Somehow. How do you convert the final S into Systematically? First of all, by being clear on what it is you want to do with the data generated by the self-assessment exercise.

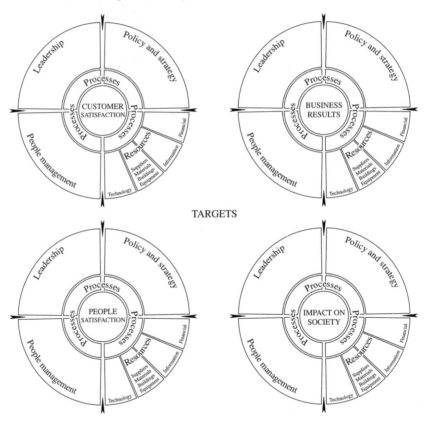

Figure 11.1   Hitting the right bull's-eyes

Targeting for best effect

A detailed self-assessment exercise is an absorbing, exciting and time-consuming process, so it is hardly surprising if on occasion a management team loses sight of its purpose. All too often, having completed the self-assessment exercise, the management team has in its possession a 'goldmine' of improvement ideas and opportunities but little idea of where to start making use of it.

During the exercise it can be easy to forget that the purpose of self-assessment is not to produce a benchmark score – although such a score is of course useful – but to analyse what the company or business unit is actually doing to improve its business performance. So rather than being regarded as just an activity 'hit-list', the findings of the self-assessment exercise should be treated as the building blocks of a business performance improvement strategy.

What we mean by a business performance improvement strategy is a strategy to create value for stakeholders. By adapting the European Business Excellence Model this can be shown graphically (see Fig. 11.2).

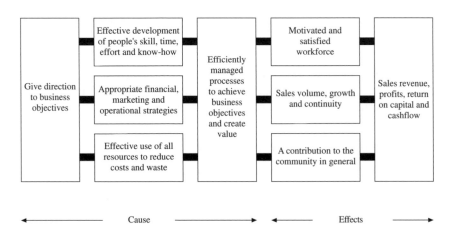

Figure 11.2 A strategic framework for creating stakeholder value

Overlaying the self-assessment findings onto this template will help managers better to understand how the identified strengths and areas for improvement fit together and contribute to a business performance improvement strategy. But this form of analysis does not, on its own, target the priorities for action that will increase stakeholder value.

Before producing an action plan to tackle the improvement opportunities identified through self-assessment, you need to be sure that you have in place relevant measurements of the effects of improvement activities undertaken throughout the organization. The existence of performance measurements aligned to the results criteria is vital if the business performance improvement strategy is to hit the right 'bull's-eyes' (see Fig. 11.3).

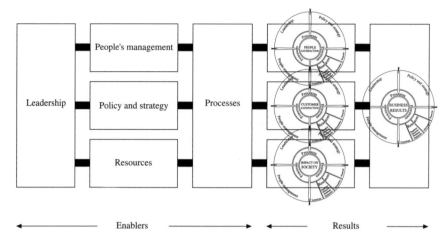

Figure 11.3   Targeting for best effect

Companies need to develop their own performance scorecard which balances in a single report both financial and non-financial measures of business performance as judged by the stakeholders.

A balanced performance scorecard

Why do companies need a new scorecard to measure performance? Because in today's fast-moving competitive environment, managers need to know how well they are creating future value. However, traditional financial measures reflect transactions that have already occurred. As Professor Robert Kaplan[1] of Harvard Business School has pointed out, many of the things that will create long-term value (e.g., research and development spending, employee training, business process improvement activity, environmental management systems) may actually cause short-term financial reports to show flat or declining performance. The reason is that traditional financial management systems measure only the expenses and the value created. Therefore, excellent companies are increasingly using a balanced scorecard of performance to identify and display the key factors that drive future values. To quote Kaplan:

> There's no single measure that adequately summarises the kind of targets and goals that create future value. Instead, the solution is a balanced set of measures. That doesn't mean hundreds of measures. In a balanced scorecard, each business selects a set of measures to track the key drivers of its current and future financial performance.

Each company needs to develop a scorecard tailored to its own situation. Based on the pioneering work of Kaplan and others, a common scorecard framework has begun to emerge, covering four broad categories of measures:

- *Financial*: shareholder value and satisfaction
- *Customer*: customer satisfaction and market performance
- *Internal business*: technology capability, manufacturing excellence, design productivity, process efficiency, etc.
- *Innovation and learning*: product, market and process innovation, etc.

This is a dynamic approach which embraces a wide spectrum of non-financial as well as financial performance measures. However, the resulting scorecard can be a complex mixture of effect-related measures and cause-related measures that may, in practice, obscure cause and effect linkages. It is not uncommon for companies to lump together both enablers and results under the internal business and innovation and learning categories.

We suggest that most business organizations will benefit from adopting a balanced scorecard approach, based squarely on effect-related measures. This requires a clear insight into what causes stakeholder satisfaction in your company and the links between cause and effect.

Because the whole purpose of developing this kind of scorecard is to create a factual basis for steering a relevant (for your stakeholders that is) business improvement strategy; not a balanced management monitoring system *per se*.

The long-standing notion of 'what gets measured gets managed' is being supplanted as static notions of command and control are swept aside by the challenges of leading almost continual change in business structures and practices. Management teams are now more concerned with measuring the effectiveness of business transformation activities, whether they be process re-engineering, best practice benchmarking or employee empowerment. They keep asking, 'Are we taking the right actions to produce the right results?'

Cause and effect

To answer the above question you need to be sure that you have in place not only relevant measurements of stakeholder satisfaction but also a mechanism to feed back the measurements into the business performance improvement planning process. The flow of performance measurement feedback to guide improvement action is illustrated in Fig. 11.4.

The causes of customer satisfaction and dissatisfaction, of people satisfaction and dissatisfaction, of societal satisfaction and dissatisfaction, as well as the drivers of business results, all need to be identified, quantified

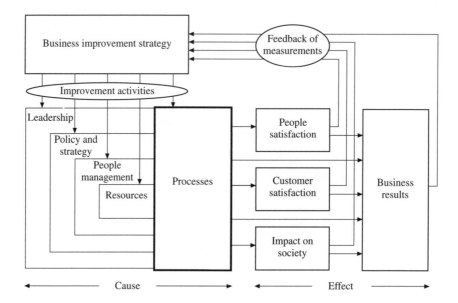

Figure 11.4   Business improvement performance feedback

and prioritized for appropriate action. The resulting parameters must be measured and, over time, trends established. The importance of using performance measures to determine improvement activities cannot be overstressed. The feedback from the results criteria sets the improvement agenda. The analysis of strengths and improvement opportunities identify from within the enabler criteria the areas for action; areas that will facilitate or constrain meeting the targets arising from the performance results feedback.

Processes are at the heart of any organization's performance improvement activities. They provide the means of harnessing peoples' energies and talents to improve business performance. If you know which processes are critical to business success and you can measure them, you have a basis for building on the leadership skills of your managers, the relevance of your policy and strategy, the know-how and talents of your people and the efficient application of your resources, so as to realize excellent approaches and their fullest deployment. Therefore, the choice of process performance measurements is critical; they should relate to and be conditioned by the stakeholder-related measurements.

The resulting business improvement strategy should focus on a few key objectives aimed at those areas of the enablers criteria that will have greatest impact on the results criteria, and consequently on business excellence.

Developing a value performance scorecard

The results criteria of the European Business Excellence Model provide a sound basis on which to develop a balanced performance scorecard. An outline of such a scorecard is shown in Fig. 11.5.

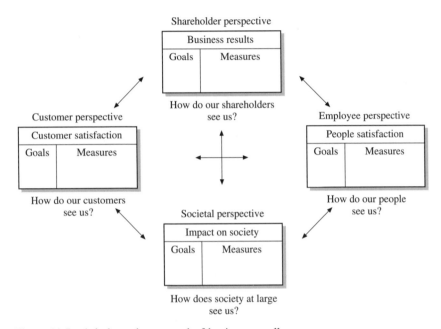

Figure 11.5 A balanced scorecard of business excellence

There is no definitive check-list of measures to which to refer when developing a performance scorecard. A company's scorecard must reflect its own specific business circumstances, although a study of the areas to address which relate to the four results criteria of the model (see Appendix) might yield some clues as to appropriate measures.

The measures adopted for customers, people and society should reflect the measures of satisfaction perceived as important by each of these stakeholder groups. Perceptions comprise three crucial elements: the expectations from the other person's viewpoint; weightings given to expectations; and their actual judgement of your performance. Clearly, if the measurements are to be an accurate reflection of value performance from the stakeholders' perspective then stakeholders must be involved in their selection.

It is not unusual to find companies analysing customer or employee satisfaction surveys (societal surveys are as yet relatively uncommon) made up of 30 to 40 measures devised by an internal research or planning function. The resulting satisfaction indices are often meaningless, because they do not reflect the reality as seen by customers or employees – the only reality worth knowing.

At a strategic level a company should seek to adopt no more than seven or eight key measures for each stakeholder group – the pulse points of value performance as seen by customers, by people and by society. Each key measure can be regarded as a critical success factor.

The effectiveness and relevance of these measures should be reviewed annually. The measures can be changed. There may be good reasons to do so: they were incorrectly selected originally, or the business might have changed due to new market opportunities, new competition, or new technology.

The measures which reflect the shareholder perspective are more clear-cut as they relate to financial parameters of created value. These are actually the base drivers of financial success and of shareholder value described in Chapter 10, namely:

- sales levels, growth and continuity
- profit as a percentage of sales
- created value as a percentage of sales
- created value per unit of pay
- created value per unit of assets
- return on invested capital
- cashflow.

The four-way matrix of value performance measures serves to shape the company's strategic direction. The strategic goals that accompany each of the measures should be stretch targets for three to five years; their achievement should lead to breakthrough performance. This in turn helps to flush out the priorities because, once the gap between where the company is today and the stretch goals established for the future is made visible, the areas for improvement required to bridge the gap become clear.

Balanced strategic planning

Strategic planning is the matching of a business's opportunities with its resources in order to develop a direction or course of action that leads to success. A stakeholder value performance scorecard adds two important extra dimensions to strategic planning:

1. *A sharper strategic focus*: By being able to test the effects of the company's strategic direction on its stakeholders, the sensitivity of the

senior management team's strategic decision-making is greatly enhanced.
2. *A better strategic alignment*: The balanced scorecard approach gives the senior management team the capability of integrating long-range strategic plans with short-term measurable objectives.

Strategic focus

In essence, strategic focus (i.e., the senior management team keeping its eye on the ball to ensure continued long-term business success) is a combination of three elements: strategic intent, core competencies and process capabilities.

Strategic intent is a company's ability to maintain a long-term commitment to competitive leadership and to create value for its stakeholders. This is very much dependent on its ability to recognize and achieve the critical success factors that have a direct influence on stakeholder satisfaction. To succeed, the strategic intent must become an obsession – a will to win – at all levels of the organization.

Core competencies are the collective learning in the organization; the collective know-how and skills that add value to a stream of multiple technologies for the benefit of customers. Hamel and Prahalad[2] argue that few companies will develop more than five or six core competencies. There are three basic tests of a core competence:

1. It provides potential access to a wide variety of markets.
2. It makes a significant contribution to the perceived customer benefit of the product or service.
3. It should be difficult for a competitor to imitate.

For example, the imaging and microelectronic know-how of Canon provided it with the competence to enter the reprographics market and challenge Xerox. Toshiba's competence in communications interfaces, display technology and rugged packaging of microcomponents was directly transferable from computer-controlled production machinery to portable computers.

Process capabilities are the company's set of key cross-functional processes which provide superior value to the customers, and thus create value for all stakeholders.

Strategic intent becomes reality through a combination of the senior management's decisions for: (a) the development of core competencies to develop new technologies and products/services; and (b) process capability for improving operational performance. By monitoring the changing perceptions of the effects of the company's strategic intent the management team is more able to focus on the enablers that facilitate its achievement.

In terms of the European Business Excellence Model, the decision-making process (policy and strategy) of the company's leaders should be focused on creating value for all the company's stakeholders through the effective management of its core competencies (the deployment of people know-how, skill, time and the use of available resources) and its business processes (see Fig. 11.6).

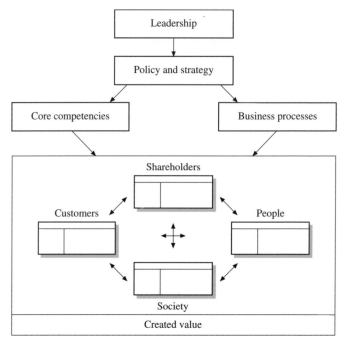

Figure 11.6   A strategic focus on creating value

The stakeholder value performance scorecard records just how effective the strategic decision-making has been.

Strategic alignment

How does the strategic intent feed down to and guide individual improvement initiatives? Planning for strategic improvement – what we have to do to improve during the next 12 months to sustain the strategic intent – is an interactive process of establishing, agreeing and deploying an annual action plan (its deployment is described in more detail in Chapter 12). A process flow of planning considerations illustrates how the value

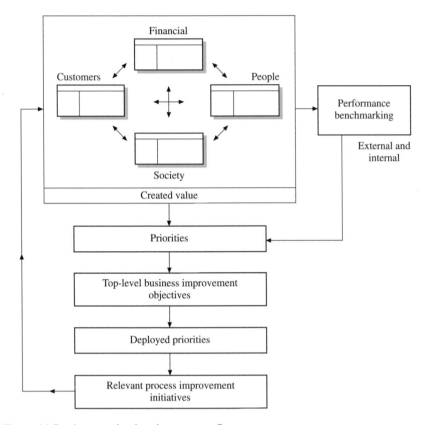

Figure 11.7   A strategic planning process flow

performance scorecard and performance benchmarking align the deployment of improvement priorities (Fig. 11.7).

Analysis of the value performance scorecard reveals if the company's
ongoing improvement actions are on target from the stakeholder's
perspective. Critical success factors comprise both a goal and a
performance measure. If the company's strategic intent is to reflect the
critical success factors held as important by the stakeholders, rather than
senior management's own, often subjective, interpretation of what is
strategically important, then a strategic goal should always be set after the
performance measure has been established.

Note that achievement against critical success factors must also be
benchmarked – externally and internally. It is important to know both the
status of the results versus external best practice and what drives the results
within the company.

Comparative customer and employee results can be evaluated by joining international performance benchmarking survey networks. Although external benchmarking of societal results is still in its infancy, many companies are members of national and regional information-sharing networks which could form the basis for a joint impact-on-society survey. Financial results can be compared against a shareholder value performance database, such as the 'Value Improvement' database based on the FT 'non-financial' index.

Internal benchmarking against the European Business Excellence Model monitors not only the company's progress against an overall operational framework of business excellence, but also its managerial capabilities: the enablers (the practices and methods) that facilitate the implementation of best practice that help it meet a critical success factor, and how it manages its core competencies and process capabilities.

The performance benchmark findings must be factored into the stakeholder value performance analysis to establish the strategic priorities for action. Experience shows that a company or business unit can realistically focus on no more than seven or eight strategic improvement objectives in one year. It is these top-level business improvement objectives that will embrace and drive all improvement actions within the organization during the coming year.

The resulting improvement projects will focus on process and competence-related activities; some will be major re-engineering projects aimed at achieving ten-fold performance breakthroughs, others will be work team created projects aimed at achieving incremental improvements; all will be contributing to a common strategic intent.

References

1. Kaplan, R.S. 'Balancing the score', in *IFS Best Practice Report 'Measuring' Performance*, pp. 19–22, IFS, Bedford, January 1995.
2. Hamel, G. and Prahalad C.K. 'Strategic intent', *Harvard Business Review*, May–June 1989, pp. 63–76.

12

Driving continuous business improvement

Experience shows that the only way of achieving world-class performance is through the creation of a company-wide framework for continuous improvement. Customer requirements and company priorities are transformed into goals for teams and individuals. Processes have to be analysed and objectives agreed at every level and at every step in the value-added chain. In the normal organizational structure, with its gaps between levels and functions, the common goal usually remains unclear. Additional links must be created to share information and to agree on priorities across functions and between levels.

Think of these links as two types of bridge:

– Bridges between levels   Policy deployment
– Bridges between functions   Process management

Policy deployment communicates and translates company objectives through successive layers in the organization. Process management communicates and translates customer requirements through successive links in the business chain. Together, they provide the structure for deciding where improvement effort will be focused (see Fig. 12.1).

Continuous business improvement is never-ending. By that we mean it is a structured year-on-year process. Each year you will, assuming you have done it properly, pass a series of milestones on your annual business improvement journey (see Fig. 12.2):

• *Planning improvement*: an annual improvement plan is created using the findings of the annual self-assessment exercise. The key priorities are identified and refined with reference to the stakeholder value performance scorecard and external performance benchmarks. The annual improvement plan supports the annual business plan.
• *Policy deployment*: the annual improvement plan is translated at each level of management into specific improvement objectives and concrete

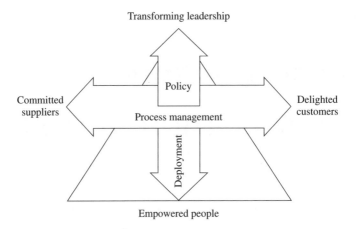

Figure 12.1   Two bridges

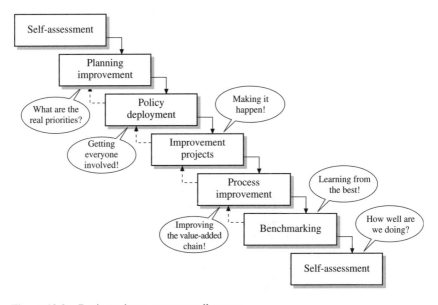

Figure 12.2   Business improvement milestones

action plans. Thus the means to achieve a particular target at one level becomes the ends for the level below.

- *Improvement projects*: the contents of the action plans are converted into improvement projects, focused on clear company priorities. Some projects will be major cross-functional activities, some will be small team improvement opportunities; all will be important.

- *Process improvement*: faces up to a fundamental challenge – maximizing the value added by a process and ensuring that it satisfies customer expectations. Process-focused management involves process control, maintenance, continuous improvement and, where necessary, radical redesign.

- *Benchmarking*: your business practices and processes against others, particularly better performing organizations, will help drive and renew your improvement strategy. Benchmarking not only provides markers by which to measure progress but also generates new ideas and inspires creativity. But you first need to be clear on what you want to improve before comparing yourself with the best.

- *Self-assessment*: is not the same as external benchmarking. Essentially, self-assessment involves the regular and systematic review of the company's strengths and weaknesses against a general model of business excellence (e.g., the European Business Excellence Model); progress towards this model of excellence should form part of the company's strategic intent.

Planning improvement

The pursuit of business excellence necessitates a clear and deployable strategic direction for business improvement, driven by priorities based on the critical success factors for business excellence. These critical success factors can be determined from the results criteria of the European Business Excellence Model, and measured accordingly (see Chapter 11 for a discussion of balanced performance scorecards).

Ideally, the business improvement strategy should incorporate a vision of business excellence at least five years into the future. The company's or business unit's five-year business excellence mission is achieved through a series of annual business improvement plans, each building on the previous one. All improvement initiatives within the organization need to be planned, linked and monitored within a structured cascade if people effort, know-how and time plus resources are to be harnessed for the overall benefit of the business and its principal stakeholders.

Successful business improvement planning and deployment, often known collectively as policy deployment, or by the Japanese term *hoshin kanri* depends on a tight focus on what is important – that means seven or eight priorities only at any one time. It also depends on a transparent planning process, unambiguous data and regular review. Therefore, an annual business improvement plan should contain no more than seven or eight business improvement goals – *real* goals which relate to a critical success factor for stakeholder value.

SMART goals

Business improvement goals should be SMART:

- *Specific* – relate to one and only one objective. The word 'and' should not appear in an objective – 'reduce cost and cycle time' are two objectives.
- *Measurable* – focus on objectives which can be quantified, e.g., reduce sales order processing time by 75 per cent within 12 months.
- *Achievable* – by the people who can best influence a successful outcome; people who are empowered to take action and are equipped with the necessary skills and resources.
- *Realistic* – take into account current priorities, and time and resource constraints. However, realistic goals reflect the realism of customer desires and competitive pressures, not internal perceptions of what is realistic. Externally focused realism sets the priorities and shifts the constraints.
- *Time-bound* – so that everyone is locked onto the current priorities, and understands not only what is required of them but by when it is required.

To set SMART goals there must be intelligent performance measures by which to monitor and steer progress.

Performance measures

The performance measures that accompany the top-level improvement objectives for the company or business unit as a whole are relatively straightforward to determine. They may be derived from a strategic business performance scorecard of the type outlined in Chapter 11.

At lower levels performance measures become more specific and demand a genuine understanding of the processes and activities targeted. This task is best left to the people who are creating their own action plans in response to deployed improvement objectives.

Good performance measures must achieve the following:

- Reflect the critical aspects of functional performance – meaningful performance measures depend on a clear understanding of functional purpose.
- Reflect the critical aspects of performance as seen by the customer – it is fundamental to establish and define the needs of both external and internal customers.

- Be understood by all those who need to understand – to be motivated people must understand the measures being used to assess their performance if they are to be held accountable.
- Be highly visible – since the prime purpose of performance measures is to inform people how well they are doing against set targets, the style of presentation is important.
- Relate to the requirements of the total business – the local performance measures should have been tested against the objectives of the overall business improvement strategy.
- Be subject to a reviewing mechanism – to ensure the continuing validity of performance measures.
- Be used in conjunction with appropriate target-setting – targets define the required rate of improvement.

The top-level improvement plan sets the direction for the coming year. Within this framework each level of the organization must develop plans and relevant performance measures to support the targeted objectives of the level above. In essence, the deployed plan focuses on the most important priority actions, ensuring that all improvement projects are tied to the future vision of the company.

Policy deployment

When the annual improvement plan has been established by top management it is translated into departmental action plans. The action plans at every given level of the company are linked to the objectives of the level above. Thus the means to achieve a particular target at one level become the ends for the level below. The measures at one level becomes the targets for the next (see Fig. 12.3).

Policy deployment is a mechanism for ensuring that everyone in the organization pulls in the same direction – towards clearly defined goals. Once objectives have been defined, critical processes can be identified (see Fig. 12.4).

Every person in the organization, therefore, becomes aware of the seven or eight key annual business improvement goals of top management and will be able to focus on the relevant process improvement activities to help accomplish the ultimate goals. Resources, therefore, are also focused on a few priority items.

At first sight this may seem like a top-down process, and, insofar that it is the top management team's responsibility for setting the overall direction of the company or business unit, yes it is. However, effective policy deployment is just as much bottom up as top down. Because at each level of deployment

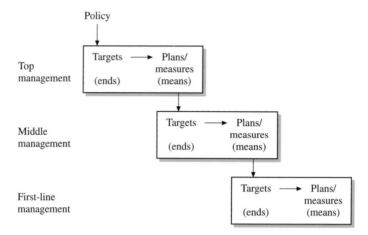

Figure 12.3   Policy deployment

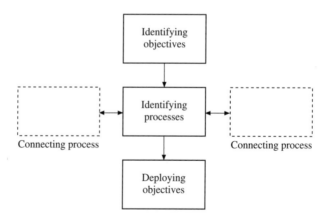

Figure 12.4   Process deployment

it is essential that there is not only a clear understanding of the overall direction but also full involvement and ownership of the action plan.

Showing people what the overall goals are and where they fit is crucial to the motivation of effective effort. People need to see that what they do makes a difference. Policy deployment focuses everyone on the most important actions that they need to undertake so as to make a real contribution to the company's overall improvement priorities.

This demands an ongoing dialogue between each level of the deployment cascade (see Fig. 12.5) during which departmental or process or team action plans are drafted. Functional managers, process owners or team leaders will,

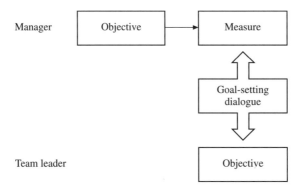

Figure 12.5 Deployment dialogue

together with their staff, translate the key business objectives into functional/process/team terms. This needs to be done in a structured, non-emotive way.

An external focus is essential to the development of all plans, even at departmental level. By looking outward at customer (probably internal customer) needs, a department will identify opportunities to contribute to customer satisfaction, and increase the amount of value-added work done. This is reinforced by the business excellence assessment feedback report which gives an overall view of the organization's strengths and areas for improvement. A department or process team may identify those assessment findings that impact on its own sphere of influence, using the information to help shape local action priorities.

The team action plan (see Fig. 12.6) is developed from three inputs:

1. the team improvement opportunities arising out of the top-level business improvement objectives
2. the opportunities to improve the service to internal customers
3. the opportunities to improve business excellence.

In order to produce a team improvement plan, the following are needed:

- the deployed business improvement objectives
- a review of the team purpose and major process tasks performed
- a review of what internal customers believe the team should be doing for them and their perceptions of the actual service received
- an analysis of the process tasks actually being performed including – from the customer's viewpoint – wasted work
- the current business excellence position report.

From these it is possible to produce an action plan with three major outputs:

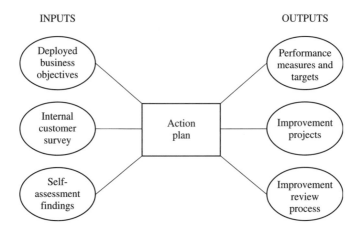

INPUTS   OUTPUTS

Figure 12.6   Team action planning

1. a set of team improvement objectives with appropriate performance measures and targets
2. a prioritized list of meaningful improvement projects based on a clear understanding of internal customer requirements, wasted work activities and the business excellence self-assessment findings
3. a highly visible team improvement review process.

The resulting action plan is discussed with the responsible manager at the next level up and refined as appropriate. This dialogue and the corresponding refinement of plans filters upwards until the top-level business improvement plan is itself refined. The finalized objectives and performance measures are then agreed and deployed for action. In this way, all improvement initiatives are aligned and owned.

Improvement projects

Experience has shown that most business improvement activities, or indeed any specific piece of work that involves the activity of more than one person, have a much greater chance of reaching a successful conclusion if the assignment is treated as a project. Furthermore, by converting a problem into a project it is given a tangibility through which it can claim the attention, resources and facilities necessary for its solution. All business improvement activities should be organized on a project management basis.

A business improvement project has certain generally recognizable characteristics:

- a specific, clearly defined problem
- clear, measurable objectives
- better managed by a team than an individual
- clear starting and finishing points
- capable of being solved through the application of a structured project management approach
- potential to contribute to stakeholder value.

Project ownership

Every project must have a project owner, usually a manager willing to sponsor (to 'champion') one or more business improvement teams in his or her own operational areas. Project ownership is a real leadership activity concerned with organizational change, and carries several crucial responsibilities which affect the success of the project. These responsibilities include the following:

- selecting appropriate projects and measurement criteria
- selecting the project team and its leader
- ensuring that the project team receives the appropriate education and training
- reviewing the progress of the project
- removing any barriers that inhibit progress; getting support from more senior managers if necessary
- communicating and rewarding success, including the recognition of individual contributions to the overall team effort.

Improvement projects are often differentiated between those that will provide significant breakthroughs to new and higher performance levels (the 'vital few') and those that will tackle the multitude of everyday improvement opportunities (the 'useful many').

Vital few type projects require ownership by a senior champion, and in some cases will be owned by the top management team. Because they are longer-term, top-down projects, the champion will have to deal with important resource and priority issues, not least of which is to ensure that day-to-day operational activities do not impede progress.

Useful many type projects need the encouragement of managers at all levels within the overall framework of the deployed business improvement plan.

Process improvement

Traditional work structures emphasize specialization, functional professionalism and departmental efficiency. Yet the key deliverables to customers that generally cross functional boundaries are often not 'owned' by anyone (see Fig. 12.7). The absence of process ownership is one of the main barriers to process improvement. The aim of process management is to improve and coordinate processes within a structure that is still functionally organized. This requires a new way of thinking – thinking *process*.

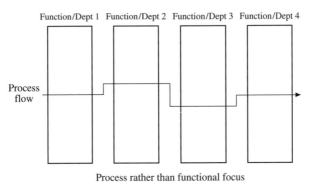

Figure 12.7 A new way of thinking

Building a process culture

Process management is more than breaking down barriers between functions. To be effective, process management depends on developing a process view of the entire business – throughout the business – around facts-based management. In other words, developing a process culture – an environment in which everyone is process focused because of the following:

- Processes are visible.
- There is a clear process structure.
- There is a framework for understanding how the business's processes provide value to customers.
- Process improvement priorities have been determined and are clearly explained.
- People are encouraged to think *process* rather than *function*.

Process management consists of several interlinked components (see Fig. 12.8):

- Process control and process maintenance form the basis for process management.
- Process control is the systematic evaluation of the performance of a process and the corrective actions taken if performance does not conform to standards.

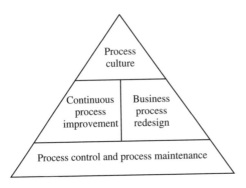

Figure 12.8   Process management

- Process maintenance assures the repeatability of processes according to standards and procedures (e.g., ISO 9000).
- Continuous process improvement is gradually but continuously improving process capabilities. Process improvement is stimulated and facilitated by management but everyone participates.
- Process redesign is the search for an implementation of radical change in business processes to achieve a breakthrough in process performance (often called 'process re-engineering'). Process redesign is the result of innovative activity carried out in addition to continuous improvement.

There is currently much debate about the respective merits of continuous incremental process improvement and radical redesign. Companies cannot achieve breakthrough competitive performance using continuous improvement alone, nor is radical redesign a fast-track substitute for continuous improvement. The two are not mutually exclusive; both are required.

A process culture aims at making the process way an important element of the prevailing attitude and behaviour of all people in the organization.

Process management

Process management focuses processes on business priorities in the following ways:

- by analysing the process structure and improving insight into cause and effect relationships
- by deploying business priorities into objectives for controlling, improving and (re)designing processes
- by establishing ownership for process control, improvement and, where necessary, stimulating the reallocation of resources.

It is relatively easy to determine what constitutes a business process; practically every work activity may be organized as a business process. The more difficult question to answer is how many processes are absolutely critical to the success of the business. The number can vary, according to the management team's perception, from as few as 4 or 5 to as many as 20 or 30 distinct processes. Most experts agree that 8 or 9 strategic processes are an appropriate number.

Strategic processes are business-wide. Each of these complex business processes is, in effect, a hierarchy of interrelated and nested subprocesses and sub-subprocesses (or work activities), as shown in Fig. 12.9.

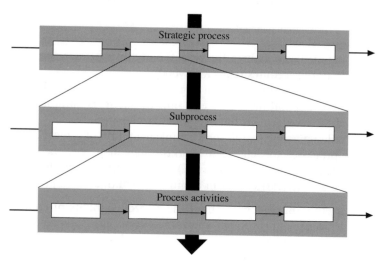

Figure 12.9   Process hierarchy

All well-managed processes have the following common characteristics:

- a process owner accountable for how well the process performs
- well-defined boundaries (a clear scope of activities)
- measurement and feedback controls close to the point where the activity takes place
- customer-related performance measures
- known cycle times.

Process owners should perform the following tasks:

- Make the process visible (mapping).
- Agree on the performance targets for the process (policy deployment).
- Measure the actual performance of the process (process control).

- Determine how well the process is meeting customer requirements (process effectiveness).
- Take measures to improve process performance as necessary (through continuous process improvement or through business process redesign).

Benchmarking

Continuous business improvement is a never-ending process requiring improvement plans to be updated annually. Benchmarking against best in class or industry leaders is an essential part of the renewal process. It not only provides milestones with which to measure progress, but also generates new ideas and inspires creativity.

The International Benchmarking Clearing House defines benchmarking as: '. . . a process of continuously comparing and measuring an organization with leaders anywhere in the world to gain information that will help it to take action to improve its performance.' Benchmarking helps drive rapid business improvement in three ways:

1. Quantifying the gap between internal and external practices creates the need for change.
2. Understanding industry best practices identifies what you must change.
3. Examination of externally benchmarked practices gives a picture of what the future holds after change.

In the words of the celebrated management guru, Sun Tzu:[1] 'If you know your enemy and know yourself, you need not fear the result of a hundred battles.' His advice, written in 500 BC, is just as relevant in today's market-place.

Types of benchmarking

There are basically three types of benchmarking:

- *Strategic*: The analysis of world-class companies in non-competitive industries to determine opportunities for strategic change initiatives. These studies are led by professionally trained benchmark analysts.
- *Performance*: The analysis of relative business performance among direct or indirect competitors. These studies focus on open-literature analysis or are conducted as 'Blind' studies using a third-party consulting firm.
- *Process*: The analysis of performance in key business processes among identified best-practice companies selected without regard to industry affiliation. Studies are conducted by teams from the process area.

Best practice benchmarking is really just another name for process benchmarking.

Preparing for benchmarking

Benchmarking starts with self-study. We must first understand ourselves before we can learn from others. Those companies which have benefited from benchmarking have learned the two crucial lessons of successful benchmarking:

1. *Define your objectives.* It is essential to know the real underlying objectives of your benchmarking project – the fundamental 'why' you want to improve. In other words, know what you are looking for and how it will affect your customers, and, therefore, your business performance.
2. *Know your own processes.* For that you need to have a process flowchart and documented systems and procedures. Very often by mapping your own processes you will see obvious improvement opportunities before you even begin benchmarking against others.

There are two halves to the basic benchmarking process: practices and metrics (see Fig. 12.10). Practices are the methods used; metrics are the quantified effect of implementing the practices. Benchmarking studies must address both sides of the equation: why? and how much?

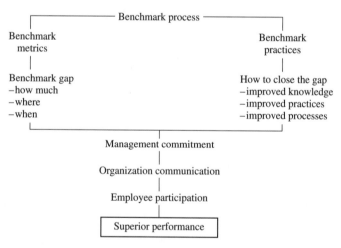

Figure 12.10   Generic benchmarking process

Benchmarking is about understanding practices. Once they are under-stood they can be quantified to show their numeric effect. Every benchmarking study project seeks to obtain the answers to six critical questions:

1. What shall we benchmark?
2. How do our internal processes work?
3. What measurements shall we apply?
4. Who shall we benchmark against and how?
5. What is the scope and nature of the performance gap?
6. How can we translate the data into real improvements?

Self-assessment

Self-assessment should be part of the annual planning cycle, updating and refining the organization's business excellence database of strengths and areas for improvement. The self-assessment findings enable the management team to keep track of the organization's progress against all the criteria and subcriteria of business excellence, and to assess the changes which occurred during the previous year. They are the platform on which the forthcoming year's priorities and action plans are shaped.

Each year the self-assessment exercise will retrace the key steps of data collection, position report, management sign-off, assessment and feedback. Having conducted a comprehensive award-style exercise once it is a lot easier to do it the second, third and fourth time around. With the benefit of experience, and a growing pool of in-house expertise, it becomes possible to manage self-assessment as a straightforward business process which, like any other business process, can be further improved and refined over time.

Data collection should not be such a challenge the second time around. Provided that a structured methodology for collecting the data has been set up, then data for collection becomes more of an information management exercise than a facts-gathering one. As self-assessment becomes established as a business process and accessible to more people within the organization, the data collection burden is no longer shared by just a few. Ultimately the whole organization will develop into a business excellence intelligence network.

Similarly, the task of writing the position report is no longer the kind of traumatic experience it was the first time around. A well-constructed and relevant position report can be transferred to a PC network so that it is converted from a passive to a proactive medium. A 'live' business excellence position report facilitates a gradual updating and refinement of the contents as the years go by, resulting in a more sensitive management tool. This also means that management sign-off becomes management sign-*on*, as senior managers take greater responsibility for the position report.

However, beware of any temptation to short-cut the assessment and feedback processes. They must be undertaken as thoroughly and as professionally as they were the first time around. An annual assessment of the position report and thoughtful feedback of the assessment findings will add value to the strategic picture and continue to extend the management team's insights into the causes and drivers of business excellence within the organization.

Reference

1. Sun Tzu. *The Art of War*, translated by Thomas Cleary, Shambhala, Boston and London, 1988.

13
The history of the European Quality Award

The European Quality Award was launched on October 1991 at the European Foundation for Quality Management's annual forum, which was held in Paris. The introduction of the award – announced at the Paris forum by European Commission vice-president, Mr Martin Bangemann – is the cornerstone of the EFQM's vision to make quality Europe's highest business goal. The award is intended to meet three fundamental objectives:

- to focus attention on business excellence in a dramatic way
- to provide a further stimulus to companies and individuals to develop business improvement initiatives
- to demonstrate the results achievable in all aspects of an organization's business activity.

As with the Deming Prize in Japan and the Malcolm Baldrige National Quality Award in the United States, there is plenty of evidence that the European Quality Award is raising the profile of business excellence as a competitive strategy not only in boardrooms but also within business schools and government circles. In an increasing number of European countries the European Business Excellence Model and the related award process has been adopted wholesale as the template for national quality awards. The UK Quality Award, for example, which was presented by Prime Minister John Major in November 1994 to the first winners, Rover Group and TNT Express, is identical to the European Quality Award.

In this chapter we deal with how the European Business Excellence Model and the European Quality Award Scheme evolved. But first we set the scene by giving an overview of the award process.

Overview of the award scheme

The procedure for making an application is described in the application brochure published annually, in five European languages, by the EFQM. Broadly, the applicant's organization prepares a written submission that addresses each of the nine criteria in the model – up to 75 pages are allowed. The submission is then forwarded to the EFQM before the closing date – sometime in March in any year. Assessment of applications is entirely independent of the EFQM. Each year the EFQM trains up to 200 managers and quality experts, selected from across Europe, in the procedure for scoring award applications. When the applications come in, teams of about six or seven assessors are assigned by the award administrators. Great efforts are made to ensure there are no conflicts of interest between the assessors and the application assigned to a particular team. Over a period of 2–3 weeks the assessors score the application. In essence, the application addresses each of the nine criteria in the model. The assessors consider the applicant's approach to each criterion from the points of view of strengths and areas for improvement. Working individually, each assessor allocates a score and completes the scorebook. Next, the team meets and, during the course of a one-day meeting, forms a team or consensus view of the application. Based on the consensus view of each application, a team of seven jurors meets to decide on the finalists. The jurors are distinguished people representing a range of European countries and interests. The present jury includes two former chief executives, two main board directors, a function director and two business school professors.

Those applicants selected as finalists receive a site visit – the team of assessors needs to verify that operations and their practice or deployment across the organization are consistent with the application document. Undoubtedly, parts of the application will require further clarification. Also, an important part of the visit is the opportunity it provides to sense the atmosphere – vital if the organization is to be regarded as a future role model.

On completion of the site visits each team prepares a final report on the applicant and the jurors meet for a second time. Their duty on this occasion is first to pick from the group of finalist organizations those to receive a European Quality Prize. Prizes are awarded to any number or all of the finalists that meet a sufficiently high level of achievement (set by the jurors). Second, the jurors select from the prize winners the organization to receive the European Quality Award. The various winners and finalists are announced at the EFQM's annual forum, which is held usually in October each year. The winner of the European Quality Award is presented with the award trophy, engraved with the winner's name and held by the winner for the year until the next forum meeting.

The award ceremony was held for the first time in 1992 and His Majesty King Juan Carlos of Spain made the presentations in Madrid. The winners were:

- European Quality Award   Rank Xerox European Division
- European Quality Prize   BOC Ltd Special Gases Division
                          Industrias del Ubierna SA-UBISA
                          Milliken European Division

In 1993 the EFQM's forum was held in Turin and Professor Umberto Colombo, Italian Minister of University Science and Technology, made the following presentations:

- European Quality Award   Milliken European Division
- European Quality Prize   ICL Manufacturing Division

In 1994, at the EFQM's forum in Amsterdam, Mr Jacques Delors, President of the European Commission, made the following presentations:

- European Quality Award   Design to Distribution Ltd
- European Quality Prize   Ericsson SA
                          IBM Semea

In 1995 Berlin was the forum venue, where Mr Juan Eguiagaray, President of the Council of Ministers of Industry of the European Union, made the following presentations:

- European Quality Award   Texas Instruments
- European Quality Prize   TNT Express

The final step in the annual process is for a feedback report to be sent to each applicant. This takes the form of a written report from the team of assessors to the applicant organization. The report concentrates on the strengths and areas for improvement picked up by the team during the course of its assessment. Its particular value is its independence – the parties involved do not have any particular axe to grind and have no possible financial gain to make from their recommendations.

A global revolution

During the last 40 years, the focus on quality has turned Japan into an economic 'powerhouse', pressuring US and European companies to respond. The result has been a global revolution affecting every facet of business. This revolution has led to the obsession that world-class companies have for business excellence.

Starting in the early 1950s, the leaders of Japan's industry turned quality into a strategic weapon. Some companies in the United States and Europe followed a similar path, but the Japanese promoted quality at all levels. Behind the promotion was the Japanese Union of Scientists and Engineers

(JUSE), in cooperation with business, government and universities. They established training courses, offered consultancy advice, employed broadcasting and used the Deming Application Prize to good effect. Quality awareness and quality values pervaded the country's economic infrastructure, helping Japan to create its own national quality movement.

The results are plain for everyone to see. Japan's use of quality as a competitive lever is well documented. For a brief overview of the Japanese approach to total quality we refer you to *The Road to Quality* by Lascelles and Dale.[1]

It is only since the end of the 1970s that quality has become a strategic issue in the United States of America. Ironically, two of the most famous internationally celebrated management gurus, Deming and Juran, were advocating the importance of quality management as a competitive weapon as long ago as the early 1950s. But, in what was basically the seller's market of the post-war world, their message went largely unheeded in their own country, the United States.

It was probably not until a now-famous television programme *If Japan can why can't we?* featuring Deming was screened in America in 1980 that quality became an issue to be addressed by American industry. Against a background of increasing Japanese automotive imports into the United States in the early 1980s and the impact on employment in the heartland of Middle America, US government and industry leaders became worried about their nation's ability to increase productivity and compete in world markets. The resulting studies of productivity and quality commissioned by the US government and special interest bodies such as the National Productivity Advisory Committee (NPAC) and the American Productivity and Quality Center (APQC) provided the impetus for the creation of a national quality campaign with a national quality award as its focal point. The net effect was to raise the profile of quality in corporate America.

Perhaps the most significant act of awareness of the implications of TQM in America has been the creation of the Malcolm Baldrige National Quality Award (see Chapter 14).

The first European companies to jump on the Total Quality bandwagon in the early 1980s were, unsurprisingly, those who first ran up against Japanese competition – companies in the automotive, electronics and domestic consumer goods industries. But, like many of the early American converts to TQM, they found that merely copying the Japanese style, while missing its substance, failed to do the trick. The early rhetoric from top executives about the importance of quality rarely translated into effective quality improvement initiatives – or results.

By the mid-1980s concern with competition and high costs was reaching crisis proportions in Europe's leading companies. There was a growing realization of just how far much of Europe's industry had fallen behind Japan and the United States: a point which was reinforced by the now world-famous MIT study, by Womack, Jones and Roos,[2] that compared world automotive manufacturers. Its conclusion was that European producers had not learned the secret of raising quality and at the same time lowering costs.

The MIT study reported that the average European large volume plant took 36.2 hours to build a car – twice the Japanese average – and produced 62 per cent more defects. US plants scored roughly midway between the two on both measures. Such negative trends were not confined to Europe's automotive industry.

It was the recurring nightmare of a single European market dominated by US and Japanese multinationals that stimulated action to help redress the balance, and led to the creation of the EFQM.

The European Foundation for Quality Management

In September 1988, the chief executives of 14 large European companies signed a letter of intent in the presence of European Commission president, Jacques Delors, to establish the EFQM as a strong driving force to enhance the competitive position of European companies in the world markets. These 14 chief executives wished to combine the experience, resources and forces of their, and other, organizations to create conditions for making quality Europe's highest business objective. To achieve this vision, two missions were proposed for the EFQM:

1. to support the management of European companies in accelerating the process of making quality a decisive influence for achieving global competitive advantage
2. to stimulate and, where necessary, assist all segments of the European community to participate in quality improvement activities and to enhance quality culture.

The EFQM's 14 founding members all rank among Europe's most important companies: Philips, Bull, Fiat, KLM, Electrolux, Volkswagen, Nestlé, British Telecom, Olivetti, Dassault, Bosch, Ciba-Geigy, Renault and Sulzer. By the end of 1995 membership of the foundation had grown to around 450 organizations. These include European companies of similar size and prestige to the founding members, e.g., ABB, Banco Bilbao Vizcaya, Daf, ICI, Pirelli and Volvo. A number of the European subsidiaries of American companies which have demonstrated a long-term economic commitment to Europe, such as 3M, American Express, Kodak, Exxon, Du Pont and IBM, have been accepted as members. In addition, a growing number of universities, business schools and consultancies have joined the foundation. Membership is drawn from organizations in all European countries.

Major conferences on TQM have been held in Montreux, London, Madrid, Turin, Amsterdam and Berlin, and have been attended by the chief executives of European companies over the last six years, and important conferences have also been held on the development of education, training and research. As a result, the EFQM today provides a leadership role for the pan-European quality management movement.

This leadership is aimed at creating a climate in which quality becomes a decisive influence in achieving global competitive advantage for European companies. To do this, it was necessary to create a focus and model for quality which, without being overly prescriptive, could act as a beacon to guide companies towards their quality goal. It was against this background that the European Quality Award came into being.

How the award was developed

Because so many people from organizations in every country within Western Europe have been involved in one form or another, the ownership of what has become known as the European TQM model is very widespread. The model is a framework for a common understanding across Europe of what TQM is all about for the managers and people working in European organizations. Indeed, such understanding is now spreading to other parts of the world. National organizations are increasingly adopting the same framework, which we prefer to call the European Business Excellence Model, and assessment processes for their own award schemes.

In this section we deal with the history of how the European Quality Award scheme evolved.

Planning the award

The EFQM's vision was to create a quality award scheme that would be perceived as the best of its kind in the world. At the start of the award's development in January 1990, how this was going to be achieved was not so clear. The development programme began with a clean sheet of paper and no preconceived view on the shape or content of the proposed award. Plenty of work on researching and gathering information had to be done before any appraisal of the pros and cons of each type of award scheme identified within Europe and elsewhere in the world could be contemplated. Analysis was made of the various attributes of each of the schemes examined and the findings were reviewed by the EFQM Steering Group Recognition (the group of EFQM member company representatives charged with overseeing the award development programme) to determine which schemes were likely to be applicable in Europe. Besides, a more clear understanding was needed of the requirements and expectations of Europeans as potential customers for this new quality award scheme.

Early in the development process the EFQM's Programme Manager, Recognition – the person responsible for managing the award development programme – met with Curt Reimann, the lead architect of the Malcolm Baldrige National Quality Award, and his colleagues at the National Institute for Standards and Technology (NIST) – the US body responsible for running the Baldrige Award. He came away convinced that it would be possible to devise and implement an award scheme for Europe within a tight time-frame that would allow the first presentations to occur in the autumn of 1992, just ahead of the launch of the European single market in January 1993.

To ensure that the first presentation of the award could be made at the 1992 EFQM forum in Madrid, some major milestones had to be achieved. It was important for the award scheme to be launched at the European Quality Forum in Paris in October 1991. This meant that the governing committee of the EFQM, who had commissioned the development of a quality award in 1989, had to have the opportunity to approve the proposed plans for its development and implementation. So at the committee's annual meeting in London, in October 1990, committee members were given an appreciation of what was likely to be involved and also the opportunity to consider in more detail some of the major issues which would be encountered. They accepted the proposal and outline plan for the award's implementation and first presentation in 1992. Most importantly, they undertook to support its satisfactory progress and to secure a means for maintaining the scheme's continuation.

Work had been proceeding since August 1990 on the determination of the criteria and the assessment model. The governing committee's decision now meant that an introduction schedule of the main activities had to be prepared.

This schedule became the basis for project management of the scheme's development. The number shown in each of the boxes in Fig. 13.1 is a reference to the more detailed project management plan.

Not all aspects of the introductory schedule are dealt with in this chapter, but we will look at a few of the major and critical ones.

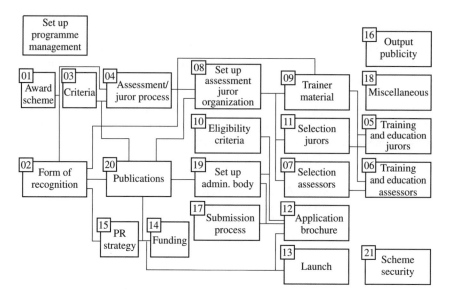

Figure 13.1   The European Quality Award development project plan
(*Source:* EFQM)

Designing the model

Returning to the criteria and the assessment model, the starting phase was researching and identifying other award schemes, such as the Deming Prize in Japan. The programme manager had already gathered much information during his discussions about the Malcolm Baldrige National Quality Award and while in the United States he had also acquired information about the NASA Excellence Award for Quality and Productivity.

The vision of the EFQM Steering Group Recognition had to be taken into account along with an appreciation of what was expected of the award scheme in the European market-place.

A series of workshops were held at the EFQM representatives' meeting in Amsterdam in June 1990. These workshops proved to be a useful basis for the formulation of expectations and therefore a framework of potential customer requirements to work against.

In early July 1990, organizations running or contemplating running award schemes in Europe were invited to attend a workshop in Brussels in August. These were mainly the national quality organizations that belonged to the European Organization for Quality (EOQ). About 50 Europeans who had in some way or other identified themselves as practising professionals of

TQM were also invited. In the event, 14 participants assembled in the Sheraton Hotel, Brussels Airport, for a three-day workshop.

The Brussels workshop started work first by addressing the question, 'What generic criteria will best judge the excellence of overall company organizations in the year 2000?' Most participants were familiar with what companies were doing or were about to do in 1990. However, they all felt that the workshop needed to focus on the future and to determine a challenging set of criteria more demanding than those currently satisfied by the best in the field. By doing so they saw that they were setting a new framework of an understanding of excellence and a vision to which businesses could aspire.

After the workshop there were several iterations of defining the top-level criteria. In December 1990 a cascade exercise of further refining and defining the criteria began. This exercise brought into play some more people for the first time. Teams worked on each of the nine top-level criteria definitions and formulated a set of what were subsequently called subcriteria, or criterion parts, plus a list of areas to address similar to those of the Baldrige Award requirements. The outcome of this exercise, so-called 'Draft 3', was then sent to about 250 people including business leaders, managers, TQM practitioners, academics and consultants from across Europe.

The circulation of Draft 3 generated numerous comments and opportunities for improvement which, over the next four months, led to a refined draft endorsed by the Steering Group Recognition in May 1991. By this time the conclusion had been reached that a set of detailed prescriptive requirements would not be used to describe what an application submission for the award should cover. The view was taken that by not being overly prescriptive, more added value would eventually be derived by organizations in their understanding and practice of Total Quality.

Bearing in mind the year 2000 factor, it was felt that the award scheme should take into account two other very important features. First, organizations truly practising Total Quality should be already undertaking regular self-appraisal. Second, the burden for organizations making an application for the Award should be minimized.

Launching the award

A name was needed for the award scheme. So a small competition was run. The very wide group of people then involved in the award's development were invited to submit their suggestions: 86 different names were received from 68 people. The most popular was the one which was chosen, the European Quality Award, with some 15 people suggesting this name. The second most popular was the European Quality Prize, which was also incorporated within the scheme. Mr Paul Malyon won the competition by suggesting these two names in the correct choice order.

The European Quality Award trophy was one of more than 30 designs submitted to the EFQM as a result of an advertisement placed in some Dutch magazines in 1990. The advertisement invited artists and designers to submit their ideas of a suitable trophy for the leadership award which the EFQM introduced in that year. Several of those involved in adjudicating the submissions saw the merit of one featuring a spherical design as ideally representing a global approach to TQM in any organization. The Steering Group Recognition favoured this design for the European Quality Award and a decision was reached in June 1991 to adopt it with the consent of the artist, Rudolf Roelofs of Amsterdam.

The award trophy is held by the winner of the European Quality Award for one year and passes on to the winner in the following year providing there is one. However, a winner of the award receives a replica of the trophy as a keepsake.

The European Quality Prize takes the form of a hologram based around the design of the award trophy. The prize winners retain their holograms.

One of the issues that concerned many people associated with developing the award scheme was how suitable assessors could be found to undertake the assessments of the applications submitted. The forecast for the first year was for some 100 assessors. The assessors would be primarily managers from European organizations. A suitable profile was prepared and chief executives of EFQM and non-EFQM companies were invited to submit nominations for people whom they thought were capable of meeting and performing the requirements.

Over 200 nominations were received of which eventually 176 applied. A selection process was used to ensure that candidates with the widest international representation of skills, experience and nationality were invited to undertake the training. Of the 106 people invited to attend the training, 100 were successfully trained.

Having recruited the potential assessors they then had to be trained. In November 1991 several leading training institutions were invited to offer volunteers to help. A meeting of about 20 training experts was held in Brussels on 2 December 1991. It was agreed at the meeting that the training would be based on a case study. The case study would be in the form of a fictitious application for the award. The whole basis of the training would be for the potential assessors to score the case study initially, then afterwards to meet in syndicate groups and debate the various criteria in the award assessment model.

As a consequence of this form of training, it was foreseen that the potential assessors would have a much more thorough understanding of the model and of the scoring system. They would therefore be much more consistent in their approach to marking applications.

The Dutch company Berenschot had already been contacted to help with the preparation of the first case study. But work on this kind of product could not be done in isolation. Several people had to read the case study and improve it each time so that salient points could be brought out during the training. The improvement work was done through three or four iterations of review and revision. The EFQM's first case study, Eurocar BV, was written initially by Vinayak Vaishnav of Berenschot BV.

In order to have a basis for interactive discussions after each of the syndicate exercises, it was decided to produce a model answer. The model answer was to serve as a common base for each of the debates that would occur in all of the training courses.

A pilot training course was held prior to the training courses for potential assessors. The pilot course involved members of the EFQM, the Steering Group Recognition and Executive Committee. This enabled the course leaders to test the case study as well as the whole training process with a view to identifying any opportunities for improvements. The team involved in conducting the training was selected from the group of 20 experts who met in Brussels at the beginning of December 1991. Six training courses were held in Brussels in successive weeks between 5 March and 9 April 1992. The result was over 100 trained award assessors.

To ensure equity and credibility for the award, it was decided to have a panel of jurors who could reach decisions based on the findings of the assessors. Again, a profile was prepared against which people were sought to provide an international blend of excellent highly qualified professionals all equipped with a broad knowledge and experience of TQM.

The jurors are a group of distinguished individuals from different European countries and professions. In 1992–94, the jury consisted of two former chief executives, two main board directors, two senior managers and two university professors. The chairman of the jury for 1992 and 1993 was Mr J. de Soet, past President of KLM (The Netherlands) and one of the founders of the EFQM. In 1994, he was succeeded by Mr Gunnar L. Johansson.

Soon after the assessor training was completed, teams were assembled to assess the award applications received by the EFQM. There were three key dates.

The first date was mid-June 1992 when the jurors would meet for the first time. By this time each of the applications had to have been assessed and the consensus reports produced so that the jurors could determine which of the applicants was to receive a site visit, if any.

The second key date was mid-September 1992 when the jurors were to select which of the site-visited applicants were to become prize winners and who, if any, was going to receive the award.

The third key date was 15 October 1992, the first day of the EFQM forum at which the awards were to be made by King Juan Carlos of Spain. All of the steps in the composite process for the award 1992 had to be finished by then.

Needless to say, all of the tasks were completed by the planned dates.

References

1. Lascelles D.M. and Dale B.G. *The Road to Quality*, IFS, Bedford, 1993.
2. Womack J.P., Jones D.T. and Roos D. *The Machine That Changed the World*, Harper Collins, London, 1991.

14
Other major quality awards

The European Quality Award is not the only major quality award. Others include Japan's Deming Prize and the Malcolm Baldrige National Quality Award in the United States. Many other countries have their own national quality awards too, including the newly launched UK Quality Award.

While these awards do have differing criteria, they share with the European Quality Award a significant common factor: they set demanding criteria which provide a template of genuine world-class standards.

This chapter concentrates on the national quality awards of Japan and the United States: the Deming Prize and the Malcolm Baldrige National Quality Award.

The Deming Prize

The Deming Prize has been awarded annually since its inception in 1951. It is managed by the Union of Japanese Scientists & Engineers (JUSE). The purpose of the Deming Prize is to '... award prizes to those companies which are recognised as having successfully applied company-wide quality control based on statistical quality control and which are likely to keep up with it in the future.'

In addition to companies, specific company divisions, factories and individuals can also win the prize. There is also a Deming International Award for Overseas Companies of which there have been only two winners to date: Florida Power & Light in 1988 and Philips Taiwan in 1991.

The Deming Prize criteria comprise ten items:

1. *Company policy and planning* How the policy for management, quality and quality control is determined and transmitted throughout all sectors of the company are examined together with the results being achieved. Whether the contents of the policy are appropriate and clearly presented are also examined.

2. *Organization and its management*   Whether the scope of responsibility and authority is clearly defined, how cooperation is promoted among all departments, and how the organization is managed to carry out quality control are examined.

3. *Quality control education and dissemination*   How quality control (QC) is taught and how employees are trained through training courses and routine work in the company concerned and the related companies are examined. To what extent the concept of QC and statistical techniques are understood and utilized, and the activeness of QC circles are examined.

4. *Collection, transmission and utilization of information on quality*   How the collection and dissemination of information on quality from within and outside the company are conducted by and among the head office, factories, branches, sales offices, and the organizational units are examined, together with the evaluation of the organization and the systems used, and how fast information is transmitted, sorted, analysed and utilized.

5. *Analysis*   Whether or not critical problems regarding quality are properly grasped and analysed with respect to overall quality and the existing production process, and whether the results are being interpreted in the frame of the available technology are subject to scrutiny, while a check is made on whether proper statistical methods are being used.

6 *Standardization*   The establishment, revision and rescission of standards and the manner of their control and systematization are examined, together with the use of standards for the enhancement of company technology.

7. *Control* ('Kanri')   How the procedures used for the maintenance and improvement of quality are reviewed from time to time when necessary are examined. Also scrutinized are how the responsibility for and the authority over these matters are defined, while a check is made on the use of control charts and other related statistical techniques.

8. *Quality assurance*   New product development, quality analysis, design, production, inspection, equipment maintenance, purchasing, sales, services and other activities at each stage of the operation, which are essential for quality assurance including reliability, are closely examined, together with overall quality assurance management system.

9. *Effects*   What effects were produced or are being produced on the quality of products and services through the implementation of QC are examined. Whether products of sufficiently good quality are being manufactured and sold is examined. Whether products have been improved from the viewpoint of quality, quantity and cost, and whether

the whole company has been improved not only in the numerical effect of quality and profit, but also in the scientific way of thinking of employers and employees and their heightened will to work are examined.

10. *Future plans*   Whether the strong and weak points in the present situation are properly recognized and whether the promotion of QC is planned in the future and is likely to continue are examined.

The criteria are subdivided into 63 particulars (or subjects for consideration). These are listed in full in Annexe 1 to this chapter. No detailed guidance is given to the applicant on the scoring criteria or to the weighting given to each section.

Prior to 1964, the Deming Prize focused on the application of statistical techniques in the factory. In 1964, however, new guidelines were applied which broadened the focus to company-wide (or total) QC. The prize then became much harder to win. Komatsu, the earth-moving equipment manufacturer, was the first company to win under the new guidelines.

The focus of the Deming Prize very much reflects the Japanese approach to managing quality – the rigorous application of techniques to locate, analyse and eliminate defects through teamwork. To win the Deming Prize companies must be prepared to put in place a huge quality bureaucracy, write an application of up to 1000 pages and spend several years working with consultants from JUSE, which administers the prize. For example, Florida Power & Light – the first non-Japanese winners – are reported to have spent over 800 000 US dollars on fees to Japanese consultants.

Deming Prize applications are typically around 1000 pages long but, when NEC Toko-Ku Ltd (a manufacturer of telephone and computer peripherals) won the prize in 1989, its documentation totalled over 24 000 pages. Just the formal presentation to the judges from JUSE ran to 300 pages of densely printed data.

No Japanese company would dream of entering the competition without signals from JUSE that it had a good chance of receiving a prize. JUSE allocates consultants to help companies implement a Total Quality Control (TQC) strategy focused on the JUSE formula.

These same experts also serve as Deming Prize judges. Unlike most other awards, however, there does not appear to be any formal training for assessors for the Deming Prize. Consequently, it is unclear how the judges' assessments are normalized.

In many ways, pursuit of the Deming Prize is more of an apprenticeship than a competition. The approach has much to do with the Japanese concern for harmony and consensus. JUSE's role is to ensure a consistent approach to TQC throughout Japanese industry. JUSE has developed an extensive infrastructure for delivering TQC education, training and consultancy. Throughout its existence the Deming Prize has helped to reinforce this consistency of approach.

The Malcolm Baldrige National Quality Award

The Malcolm Baldrige National Quality Improvement Act, signed by President Reagan on 20 August 1987, established an annual US quality award. The award is named after a former US Secretary of Commerce in the Reagan Administration. Its purpose is to promote quality awareness, to recognize the quality achievements of US companies and to publicize successful quality management and improvement strategies. The US Department of Commerce and the NIST are responsible for administering the scheme.

Up to two awards can be given each year in each of three categories: manufacturing companies or subsidiaries, service companies or subsidiaries and small businesses (independently owned and with not more than 500 employees). The recipients receive a specially designed gold-plated medal set in crystal. They may publicize and advertise their awards provided they agree to share information about their successful quality management and improvement strategies with other US organizations.

Award winners from 1988 to 1994 are listed in Table 14.1.

Entries for the Baldrige Award are assessed and scored by teams of 'examiners'. The examiners are drawn from industry, government agencies, the military, academia and consultancies.

Every Baldrige Award application is evaluated in the following seven major categories with a maximum total score of 1000 points:

1.0   Leadership
2.0   Information and analysis
3.0   Strategic planning
4.0   Human resource development and management
5.0   Process management
6.0   Business results
7.0   Customer focus and satisfaction

Their relationships are illustrated in Fig. 14.1. The full list of 7 categories and 24 items and their respective scoring weights are given in Annexe 2 to this chapter.

Table 14.1 1988–94 Baldrige Award winners

Year	Manufacturing	Small business	Service
1988	Motorola Westinghouse Electric, Commercial Nuclear Fuel Division	Globe Metallurgical	
1989	Milliken & Company Xerox Business Products & Systems		
1990	GM Cadillac Motor Car Division IBM Rochester	Wallace Co.	Federal Express
1991	Solectron Corporation Zytec Corporation	Marlow Industries	
1992	AT&T Network Systems Group Texas Instruments Defense Systems & Electronics Group	Granite Rock Company	AT&T Universal Card Services Ritz–Carlton Hotel Company
1993	Eastman Chemical Company	Ames Rubber Corporation	
1994		Wainwright Industries	AT&T Consumer Communications Service GTE Directories Corporation

Each application for the Baldrige Award is evaluated on three dimensions:

- *Approach* What strategy and methodology does the company use to achieve world-class quality?
- *Deployment* What resources are being applied, and how widespread is the quality effort in the company?
- *Results* Is there convincing evidence of sustained improvement?

The Baldrige scoring guidelines matrix is shown in Table 14.2.

Finalists are subjected to 350–400 hours of evaluation by an average of 6 expert examiners, including 4-day site visits. Quantitative results weigh heavily in the judging process, so applicants must be able to prove that their quality efforts have resulted in sustained improvements. The thoroughness

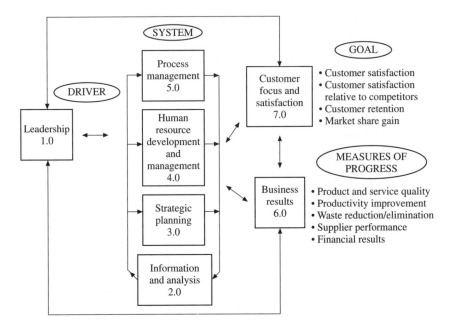

Figure 14.1   Malcolm Baldrige Award framework
(*Source:* National Institute of Standards and Technology)

of the judging process means that even applicants not selected as finalists get valuable feedback on their strengths and weaknesses.

US companies often assess their chances of winning before actually entering the competition by conducting an internal audit using the current application guidelines and evaluation criteria.[1] Some large companies rate their chances of success by holding interdivisional competitions based on the Baldrige evaluation criteria and nominating the winner as the Baldrige entry.

The UK Quality Award

Launched in 1994, the UK Quality Award is open to all organizations – whether in the private, public or voluntary sectors – who can 'demonstrate that their approach to Total Quality Management has contributed significantly to satisfying the expectations of customers, employees, shareholders and other stakeholders'. Administered by the British Quality Foundation (BQF), the UK Quality Award is consistent in all respects with the European Quality Award; it uses the same business excellence model, self-assessment and award application and judgement processes. The BQF is

Table 14.2   Baldrige Award scoring guidelines

Score (%)	Approach	Deployment	Results
0	Anecdotal, no system evident	Anecdotal	Anecdotal
10–40	Beginnings of systematic prevention basis	Some to many major areas of business	Some positive trends in the areas deployed
50	Sound, systematic prevention basis that includes evaluation/ improvement cycles Some evidence of integration	Most major areas of business Some support areas	Positive trends in most major areas Some evidence that results are caused by approach
60–90	Sound, systematic prevention basis with evidence of refinement through improvement cycles Good integration	Major areas of business From some to many support areas	Good to excellent in major areas Positive trends – from some to many support areas Evidence that results are caused by approach
100	Sound, systematic prevention basis refined through evaluation/ improvement cycles Excellent integration	Major areas and support areas All operations	Excellent (world-class) results in major areas Good to excellent in support areas Sustained results Results clearly caused by approach

working alongside the EFQM to ensure the parallel development of both award schemes.

In its first year the award was open only to 'for profit' organizations. Its first winners were the Rover Group and TNT Express, who received their awards from Prime Minister John Major in November 1994.

The scope of the award has since been widened to include 'not for profit' organizations in the public and voluntary sectors. Applicants may also be foreign-owned organizations, provided that they have a substantial presence in the United Kingdom.

Both of the award categories (businesses and public and voluntary service organizations) are subdivided into those with greater or less than 250 employees. There is no distinction in the status of award winners between the categories, and no overall winner. Entrants in each category are judged in exactly the same way against the excellence model which forms the basis of the award. It is unlikely that the total number of awards will be high as the objective is to recognize exceptional and outstanding levels of achievement.

The UK Quality Award is intended as a catalyst to hasten the spread of best Total Quality practice through all types of organization in the United Kingdom. Its scope will develop. The introduction of regional, local and sectoral awards is being encouraged.

Deming, Baldrige and European Quality Awards compared

A direct comparison between the three major awards is not really possible given the fundamental differences in their structure. But it is probably worth recording these differences and their emphases. Before attempting to highlight the contrasts between the awards we should recognize that each is a product of its 'generation'.

The Deming Prize was launched in 1951, with the declared purpose of 'Awarding Prizes to those companies recognised as having applied Company Wide Quality Control based on statistical quality control'. It was introduced at a time when Japanese industry was being encouraged to apply the then new tools of scientific management to improve quality and productivity. Thus the theme of the prize was overwhelmingly one of statistical methods and quality improvement tools and techniques – and, in essence, it remains so today.

To Western eyes the basic tenets of the Deming Prize – meticulous process measurement, systematic control, scientific problem-solving, incremental improvement, quality assurance – may appear somewhat introspective when set against today's wider perspective of business excellence based on stakeholder value. However, the impact of the Deming Prize and the power of its principles should not be underestimated. The leading Japanese companies cannot be accused of neglecting the interests of their customers, their people, their investors or society for that matter.

Although the Malcolm Baldrige National Quality Award was launched in 1987, many of its underlying principles originated in the early 1980s as a reaction to Pacific Rim competition. The declared purpose of the Baldrige Award was to 'Promote quality awareness, recognise quality achievements of US companies, and publicise successful quality strategies'.

It is very much concerned with the implementation of a company-wide system of TQM, and is supported – unlike the Deming Prize – by detailed assessment check-lists and documentation. Award applicants, and those organizations using the Baldrige system for self-assessment purposes, have a clear understanding of what is expected of them.

The Baldrige criteria have been refined considerably since 1988. While the basic structure of seven categories has remained unchanged, there have been shifts of emphasis in meaning and relative scoring weights. Take category 3.0 for example. In 1989, this category was called 'Planning for quality' (and accounted for a maximum of 80 points out of 1000); in 1990 it became 'Strategic quality planning' (up to 90 points); and in 1995 it became 'Strategic planning' (down to 55 points).

Two other categories which used to have a definite quality bias have shifted subtly towards a wider definition of business excellence: category 5.0 has evolved from 'Quality assurance of products and services' to 'Process management'; category 6.0 from 'Quality results' to 'Business results'. It is the change in the last category which is probably the most significant. Until 1995 the maximum score for 'Customer satisfaction' (now 'Customer focus and satisfaction') was 300 points out of 1000, weighted twice as heavily as any other category. Then in 1995 category 6.0 was renamed 'Business Results' and increased in weighting from 150 to 250 points (the same as the new points' weighting for 'Customer focus and satisfaction'). This may signal a gradual change in emphasis for Baldrige from a TQM system model to a business excellence model more akin to that of the European Quality Award.

The European Quality Award reflects a 1990s focus on a holistic approach to managing business excellence. By splitting the award criteria into enablers and results, equal weighting is given to cause and effect. It is impossible to win the award without being a successful company as well as an excellently managed one. The award clearly defines success as in both financial and non-financial terms – for a variety of stakeholders. Indeed the European Business Excellence Model (which also underpins the UK and other national excellence awards) is, so far, unique in that it explicitly recognizes the impact on society of managerial actions.

Importantly, the European Business Excellence Model has a visual integrity and impact which for many people provides a powerful symbol and an insight into how business excellence operates and can be managed.

Reference

1. National Institute of Standards and Technology. *The Malcolm Baldrige National Quality Award 1995 Award Criteria*, NIST, Gaithersburg.

Annexe 1   Check-list for the Deming Application Prize

Item	*Particulars*
1. Policy	(1) Policies pursued for management, quality and quality control
	(2) Method of establishing policies
	(3) Justifiability and consistency of policies
	(4) Utilization of statistical methods
	(5) Transmission and diffusion of policies
	(6) Review of policies and the results achieved
	(7) Relationship between policies and long and short-term planning
2. Organization and its management	(1) Explicitness of the scopes of authority and responsibility
	(2) Appropriateness of delegations of authority
	(3) Interdivisional cooperation
	(4) Committees and their activities
	(5) Utilization of staff
	(6) Utilization of QC Circles activities
	(7) Quality control diagnosis
3. Education and dissemination	(1) Education programs and results
	(2) Appropriateness of delegations of authority
	(3) Teaching of statistical concepts and methods, and the extent of their dissemination
	(4) Grasp of the effectiveness of quality control
	(5) Education of related company (particularly those in the same group, subcontractors, consignees and distributors)
	(6) QC circle activities
	(7) System of suggesting ways of improvements and its actual conditions
4. Collection, dissemination and use of information on quality	(1) Collection of external information
	(2) Transmission of information between divisions
	(3) Speed of information transmission (use of computers)
	(4) Data processing, statistical analysis of information and utilization of the results
5. Analysis	(1) Selection of key problems and themes
	(2) Propriety of the analytical approach
	(3) Utilization of statistical methods
	(4) Linkage with proper technology
	(5) Quality analysis, process analysis
	(6) Utilization of analytical results

		(7)	Assertiveness of improvement suggestions

6. Standardization

(1) Systematization of standards
(2) Method of establishing, revising and abolishing standards
(3) Outcome of the establishment, revision or abolition of standards
(4) Contents of the standards
(5) Utilization of statistical methods
(6) Accumulation of technology
(7) Utilization of standards

7. Control

(1) Systems for the control of quality and such related matters as cost and quantity
(2) Control items and control points
(3) Utilization of such statistical control methods as control charts and other statistical concepts
(4) Contribution to performance of QC circle activities
(5) Actual conditions of control activities
(6) State of matters under control

8. Quality assurance

(1) Procedure for the development of new products and services (analysis and upgrading of quality, checking of design, reliability, and other properties)
(2) Safety and immunity from product liability
(3) Process design, process analysis, and process control and improvement
(4) Process capability
(5) Instrumentation, gauging, testing and inspecting
(6) Equipment maintenance, and control of subcontracting, purchasing and services
(7) Quality assurance system and its audit
(8) Utilization of statistical methods
(9) Evaluation and audit of quality
(10) Actual state of quality assurance

9. Effects

(1) Measurement of results
(2) Substantive results in quality, services, delivery time, cost, profits, safety, environment, etc.
(3) Intangible results
(4) Measures for overcoming defects

10. Planning for the future

(1) Grasp of the present state of affairs and the concreteness of the plan
(2) Measures for overcoming defects
(3) Plans for further advances
(4) Linkage with the long-term plans

Annexe 2   The Malcolm Baldrige National Quality Award examination criteria

1995 Examination categories/Item	*Point values*
1.0 Leadership	**90**
1.1 Senior executive leadership	45
1.2 Leadership system and organization	25
1.3 Public responsibility and corporate citizenship	20
2.0 Information and analysis	**75**
2.1 Management of information and data	20
2.2 Competitive comparisons and benchmarking	15
2.3 Analysis and uses of company-level data	40
3.0 Strategic planning	**55**
3.1 Strategy development	35
3.2 Strategy deployment	20
4.0 Human resource development and management	**140**
4.1 Human resource planning and evaluation	20
4.2 High-performance work systems	45
4.3 Employee education, training and development	50
4.4 Employee well-being and satisfaction	25
5.0 Process management	**140**
5.1 Design and introduction of products and services	40
5.2 Process management: product and service production and delivery	40
5.3 Process management: support services	30
5.4 Management of supplier performance	30
6.0 Business results	**250**
6.1 Product and service quality results	75
6.2 Company operational and financial results	130
6.3 Supplier performance results	45
7.0 Customer focus and satisfaction	**250**
7.1 Customer and market knowledge	30
7.2 Customer relationship management	30
7.3 Customer satisfaction determination	30
7.4 Customer satisfaction results	100
7.5 Customer satisfaction comparison	60
Total points	**1000**

15
What it takes to win

Winning the European Quality Award (EQA) is an internationally respected pinnacle of achievement. Not only is a prize-winning company seen to excel in the European market-place, but also its approach to business excellence is regarded as a benchmark against which other organizations can measure their achievements and their own drive for continuous improvement. However, prestigious though the award is, for most companies there is an even greater prize: sustained business growth and value. A prize-winning company will be able to demonstrate both over a period of years. Most organizations will probably never apply for an award, but their aim is the same as an award applicant: to be among the best. To be a winner requires an organization to perform well against the same underlying criteria; those of the European Business Excellence Model.

This concluding chapter looks at what distinguishes the top-performing companies – the winners – from the rest, and outlines some common characteristics. But simply copying the winning approaches of another organization will not bring about success. Every business enterprise and its culture is unique, so each organization must work out its own routemap for success. This is what is meant by the phrase, 'becoming a learning organization'. Winning organizations are successful at learning the keys to their business: the needs and expectations of their stakeholders, and their own organizational/managerial strengths and areas for improvement.

But first, let us consider what it takes to win the European Quality Award.

Award-winning excellence

So what would be a truly excellent company score using the European Quality Award criteria?

- Allowing for variations in assessor markings, anything between 700 and 800 is exceptional and an award-winning level today. A score of 750+ represents genuine world class.
- Anything above 600 points represents a level of excellence to which few companies can currently aspire.

- A score of 500 to 600 indicates a company that is doing the right things and is starting to pull away from the pack. A score of 500+ points suggests a likely candidate for an award site visit – a potential finalist – but not necessarily a prize winner.
- A typical score for an organization which is being managed competently and has a good set of results is around 450 points. Experience suggests that an internal self-assessment score of 450 points should be considered as the minimum needed by an organization making an award application with any realistic chance of getting a site visit.
- Many more organizations achieve or can achieve a score in the 300–400 band. Generally the score is reached by higher scoring of enablers than of results. Perceived views of customers, people and society are at the early days of measurement and are not as comprehensive as the more excellent companies. Also, business results (both financial and non-financial), are not really well advanced or well correlated with the enabler criteria of how things are being done to realize good performance against targets, particularly for processes. Breakthrough for companies at this level is likely in time, but many need help to identify what must be done to realize the greatest benefits.
- The vast majority of first-time assessments will score below 300 points. The score reflects a business that lacks the kind of coherent and consistent managerial approaches needed to drive a top-performing company, although many aspects may be systematic and reviewed (occasionally). Scores on results are usually lower than for enablers which indicates a lack of stakeholder focus, particularly customers and employees. The focus is often on short-term financial results.

A note of caution: any organization considering making a European Quality Award application, particularly if it is in the 450–500 category, should recognize that award scoring is based on a strict interpretation of the assessment guidelines. The resulting assessment could be as much as 100–150 points below a more 'friendly' assessment done internally. For more information on interpreting the requirements of the European Quality Award, we recommend the EFQM publication *Winning European Quality* by Eugene Foley.[1]

You might find it useful to compare your organization's self-assessment scores against those achieved by European Quality Award applicants in 1992 and 1993, the first two years of the award. The individual scores of the applicants have been aggregated and are displayed in Table 15.1 as percentages falling within each 10-point score band. Thus for leadership, 30 per cent of all applicants scored between 31–40 per cent of the points available.

Table 15.1 The European Quality Award applicant scores, 1992–93

Criterion	0–10%	11–20%	21–30%	31–40%	41–50%	51–60%	61–70%	71–80%	81–90%	91–100%
Leadership	0	0	8	30	27	16	19	0	0	0
Policy and strategy	0	3	16	16	30	19	8	3	5	0
People	0	0	8	27	19	22	16	8	0	0
Resources	3	3	8	11	31	14	19	11	0	0
Processes	0	3	5	22	40	14	8	8	0	0
Customer satisfaction	0	3	16	19	27	13	11	11	0	0
People satisfaction	0	11	16	24	14	14	13	8	0	0
Impact on society	0	8	11	30	19	22	5	5	0	0
Business results	0	3	8	18	30	14	11	16	0	0

Source: EFQM

General scoring trends

Below are our observations on general scoring trends. Our comments, which relate to a wide range of company and business unit assessments, not just those of the European Quality Award finalists displayed in Table 15.1, are based not only on our own experiences but also on those of many other colleagues in other consultancies, training organizations and companies engaged in carrying out assessments.

LEADERSHIP

The requirement is for leadership qualities in all people with responsibilities for others. This is generally overscored because the influence of leadership is often perceived by assessors as being the prerogative of those managers at the top. Even so, scores are not usually above 70 per cent for leadership overall.

POLICY AND STRATEGY

Often the excellence of the approach is viewed as better than 50 per cent but the deployment is usually not so high. Scores are generally higher than 35 per cent overall with some organizations scoring over 80 per cent.

PEOPLE MANAGEMENT

These scores are generally very varied with the best organizations attaining up to 75 per cent overall. But most scores overall are between 25 and 45 per cent.

RESOURCES

Scores seem to depend on the type of business, but are not usually above 75 per cent overall. Generally, organizations are not as good as they think they are about *how* they manage their resources to best effect.

PROCESSES

The best companies have process management well under control and score as high as 80 per cent. But the vast majority still have a long way to go to reach this level. Scores between 20 and 60 per cent are not uncommon.

CUSTOMER SATISFACTION

This is more likely to be what the company thinks the customer thinks (!)

although customer enquiries/surveys are on the increase. (Whatever happened to market research?) The best can show good performance against targets; their own, 'competitors' and 'best in class'. Scores are most likely today to be lower than 50 per cent overall.

PEOPLE SATISFACTION

Not well scored with too few companies not regularly measuring their people's satisfaction. A fear of bad news prevails! Again, the majority of scoring is between 35 and 50 per cent overall.

IMPACT ON SOCIETY

It is difficult for many companies to score more than 50 per cent overall because of a lack of any measurements. Generally scores are between 20 and 40 per cent.

BUSINESS RESULTS

There is varied scoring with high scores too often being given to run of the mill, legally required measures (financial). The training for this criteria has been strengthened each year since 1992, the first year of the European Quality Award. Good scores are between 50 and 65 per cent with many well down to between 20 and 40 per cent.

The set of scores for an excellent company is generally constant across all criteria, suggesting that the management of business excellence or TQM in its widest sense has been practised for longer than five years. Scores will be above 60 per cent for all criteria.

An award or prize is not given where there is no clear evidence of a direct link between results and action, and that the action was influenced by results/measures concerning the customers, investors and the workforce. Nor is one given if the future financial stability over at least two years does not look feasible to a group of financial experts. The future business plan has to be sound.

Winning business excellence

We live in an exciting era of change and opportunity. Business excellence is an approach for managing change in an environment where the accepted paradigms are subject to constant challenge. It is an approach that is concerned with developing an organizational culture in which people are able to meet these challenges and realize the opportunities of change. Business excellence is no longer a fuzzy concept bound up with a notional pursuit of perfection. Based on the simple premise that business excellence is the achievement of good results through the involvement of all employees in continuous improvement of their processes, the European model provides a very clear framework for its realization. In the right hands, business excellence becomes a powerful strategy with which to win customers and sustain a competitive edge.

In Chapter 1, we stated that independent studies have shown that the characteristics of world-class performance correspond with those of business excellence, namely:

- strong leadership
- motivated employees
- extremely high customer satisfaction ratings
- a strong and/or rapidly growing market share
- highly admired by peer group companies and society at large
- business results that put it in the upper quartile of shareholder value.

Apart from their ability to satisfy the needs and expectations of their customers and other stakeholders better than their competitors, one thing above all else seems to differentiate the winners from the losers: their ability to learn fast. While most companies understand the need to learn fast and to change fast, few know how to do it. Attempts to emulate the improvement strategies of world-class companies usually fail to deliver the promised results. What works well in one organizational culture may not succeed in another. In fact, every company must work out for itself what needs to be done to adjust the organization continuously to suit the changing circumstances it faces. The best companies know what drives success and what constitutes excellence in *their* businesses.

What the top-performing companies do appear to have in common are the following:

Farsighted, committed and involved leaders

Excellent companies understand that leadership is about coping with change, and that change – which is almost the only constant factor in business today – requires effective leadership. They have learned that the function of leadership is to bring about change by doing the following:

- Setting a direction – developing a vision of the future and charting a realistic way of getting there

- Aligning people – establishing a collective sense of purpose
- Motivating and inspiring – energizing and supporting people to make the vision a reality.

Top-performing organizations do not believe that leadership is concerned with charisma or other exotic personality traits, but with a set of skills that can be taught. Nor do they perceive leadership as the preserve of a chosen few. They go to great lengths to give as many people as possible leadership opportunities in order to develop a cadre of leaders throughout the organization. In other words, they seek to develop a *leadership culture*.

Such companies encourage all of their managers to think in boardroom terms, like investors, and to consider the long-term consequences of their decisions.

A clear understanding of their critical success factors

Top-performing companies recognize that their competitive edge is based on their ability to identify and create value for their stakeholders. Therefore, they know what is important from the perspective of each of their stakeholders: their customers, their people, their shareholders and society in general. Thus the management team has a vision of where it wants to go which is based on reality. This knowledge governs all of the decision-making and improvement activities. The priorities are related to the critical success factors that have a direct influence on stakeholder satisfaction.

Unambiguous direction setting

In top-performing companies everyone pulls in the same direction – towards clearly defined goals. Teams and individuals throughout the organization understand the overall business objectives and are able to translate these priorities into specific action plans. Successful organizations ensure not only that there is clear understanding of the overall direction but also that people have full involvement and ownership of the action plan.

In such companies direction-setting is not a one-off exercise conducted at periodic intervals but a continuing cycle of stimulating relevant action, review, refinement and renewal.

Flexible and responsive processes

World-class organizations have learned to develop a network of business processes that support their business mission. They have attempted to simplify their process structure, identifying and building on the core elements of the business which together create value for customers and other stakeholders. They have developed a *process culture* – an environment in which everyone is process focused; where people have responsibility for and ownership of processes and clearly understand cause (of process performance) and effect (on customer satisfaction) relationships; where business priorities stimulate and drive process improvement and redesign activities rather than the other way around (i.e., process capabilities do not constrain business goals – which is all too often the case).

People with relevant know-how and skill sets

Successful companies have discovered that their ability to create value is based on two foundations:

- the satisfaction and perception of customers
- the efficient combination of the resources of intellectual capital and use of financial capital.

The top-performing companies in the FT non-financial index outperform the rest of the pack by creating value from sales and from human capital. Research has shown that the most profitable companies have higher created value per unit of pay. The lower-performing companies do significantly worse in this respect. Often, companies with lower profitability have invested in financial resources but do not appear to have obtained the benefits expected (e.g., improved productivity, cost reductions or more business).

Top-performing companies do not neglect their stock of human and intellectual capital (people skills, time, effort and know-how). They recognize that it is in their people that the collective expertise (the core competencies) of the business resides. Not only do they recognize that intellectual capital is expandable through training and development, but they also ensure that their people have the means to listen to their customers needs and understand how they can personally contribute to improved business performance.

A constant searching for improvement

Winning companies are those which are able to improve at a faster rate than their competitors. They are responsive to their customers' needs and are adept at meeting them. They set stretch goals over three to five years aimed at achieving breakthrough performance. They are focused on the priorities – the performance goals – that must be achieved in order to bridge the gap between where the company is today and where it wants to be in the future.

Stretch goals demand an extraordinary learning curve. They are the catalyst that stimulates continuous improvement to take place at a revolutionary, not evolutionary, rate. World-class companies are world class because they have learned how to do this; how to encourage, support and benefit from the growth of an *improvement culture.*

An objective assessment of annual and future performance

Excellent companies base their business improvement decision-making on an objective assessment of where they are today and where they expect to be tomorrow. They clearly understand the following:

- how their company works
- how good they are
- how they compare with others
- how good they need (want) to be
- what needs changing
- where to start.

Becoming a learning organization

How does a company develop a holistic approach to achieving business excellence and success? There is no prescriptive approach. The approach taken will vary from company to company, and is derived from a process of self-learning.

Each company has to work out for itself the answers to seven key questions:

1. How does an excellent company operate and how can any organization measure its own progress?
2. What are the key drivers of business success?
3. Which are the successful companies (in value performance terms) and how can companies benchmark themselves on the critical value performance drivers?
4. How can a company/business unit measure the created value of its markets, products and processes?
5. What are the key management decision factors that affect business success?
6. How do we focus management decisions and actions on the real issues that will drive business success?
7. How do we create a structure that will link together all improvement initiatives to create value for the company's stakeholders?

We cannot simply tell you what to do – but then neither can anyone else.

Business is too dynamic to be subjected to a set of ready-made solutions. What we can do is to suggest a logical sequence of activities which, based on our experience, contribute to a company learning experience. But remember, the prime focus should be on improving stakeholder results; do not fall into the trap of implementing a company learning programme for its own sake.

A self-learning process

We have framed this sequence of activities as a four-phase self-learning process:

PHASE 1 AWARENESS

(Understanding the links between business excellence and financial success: a prerequisite for focused business improvement)

- Understand how companies create real value and how this relates to the European Business Excellence Model.
- Identify the drivers of business success and of created value in your company/business unit.
- Learn how to benchmark business excellence (through self-assessment against the European Business Excellence Model) and created value (against your industry sector, competitors and world-class performers) to help you concentrate on the right strategic priorities for your business.
- Understand how managerial decisions impact on business excellence and financial performance – a 1 per cent beneficial change in seven key management decision factors can increase profits by between 20 and 60 per cent overall.

PHASE 2 ASSESSMENT

(Strategic benchmarking: getting a corporate/business unit compass bearing)

- Determine your performance against seven key ratios of business success: sales volume, growth and continuity; profit as a percentage of sales; created value as a percentage of sales; created value per unit of pay; created value per unit of assets; return on invested capital; cashflow. Use these ratios to benchmark yourself against your industry sector, competitors and world-class performers.
- Assess your organization against the nine criteria of the European Business Excellence Model to understand fully your position today (your strengths and areas for improvement) and then use this benchmark to seek continuous improvement.

PHASE 3   ACTION PLANNING

(Deciding what to do and how)

- Use the ability to identify and measure the criteria for business excellence (namely, the European Business Excellence Model), the base drivers of business success (namely, the seven key business success ratios) and the critical management decision factors (namely, the seven 1 per cent sensitivity factors) to determine the major opportunities for business improvement.
- Create a business improvement plan to convert these opportunities into specific goals, targets and performance measures to enable everyone in the organization to concentrate their efforts where it matters.
- Establish an implementation plan to support the business-wide improvement activities.

PHASE 4   IMPLEMENTATION

(Making it happen: driving structured business improvement activity)

- Create a business-wide structure for continuous improvement which integrates the mechanisms of strategy deployment (alignment between levels) and process management (integration across functions), and which is based on sound project management.
- Deploy the business improvement plan, ensuring that it is translated by each area of the organization into specific improvement objectives and action plans.
- Convert the contents of the action plans into process improvement projects, focused on clear company priorities. Some projects will be major cross-functional activities, some will be small team improvement opportunities; all will be important.
- Improve the effectiveness and created value of all processes and, where necessary, radically redesign critical business processes.

We encourage companies to adapt this approach to their specific needs.

We are not alone in our belief that the framework of the European Business Excellence Model provides companies with a clear strategic focus. The challenge for any organization which seeks to achieve superior business performance is to:

- *Learn* how to apply this framework to create value in their business.
- *Assess* where they are now, where they need to be and how they are going to get there.
- *Plan* and *implement* an effective and relevant business improvement strategy.

Hopefully the contents of this book will have given you food for thought and some clues on how to address these issues.

Reference

1. Foley, E. *Winning European Quality*, European Foundation for Quality Management, Brussels, 1995.

Appendix
The European Business Excellence Assessment Criteria (1996)

Leadership – Criterion 1

Definition

The behaviour of all managers in driving the organization towards Total Quality.

How the executive team and all other managers inspire and drive Total Quality as the organization's fundamental process for continuous improvement.

Criterion parts

Self-assessment should demonstrate:

1A   VISIBLE INVOLVEMENT IN LEADING TOTAL QUALITY

Areas to address could include *how* managers take positive steps to:

- communicate with staff
- act as role models leading by example
- make themselves accessible and listen to staff
- give and receive training
- demonstrate commitment to Total Quality.

1B   A CONSISTENT TOTAL QUALITY CULTURE

Where a Total Quality culture is defined as the way people work and business is done in the organization within which all people clearly embrace TQM as the basis for their own activities and the further development of the organization.

Areas to address could include *how* managers take positive steps to:

- be involved in assessing awareness of Total Quality
- be involved in reviewing progress in Total Quality
- include commitment to and achievement in Total Quality in appraisal and promotion of staff at all levels.

1C TIMELY RECOGNITION AND APPRECIATION OF THE EFFORTS AND SUCCESSES OF INDIVIDUALS AND TEAMS

Areas to address could include *how* managers are involved in recognition:

- at local, section or group level
- at divisional level
- at the level of the organization
- of groups outside the organization, e.g., suppliers or customers.

1D SUPPORT OF TOTAL QUALITY BY PROVISION OF APPROPRIATE RESOURCES AND ASSISTANCE

Areas to address could include *how* managers provide support through:

- helping to define priorities in improvement activities
- funding, learning, facilitation and improvement activities
- actively supporting those taking quality initiatives
- releasing staff to participate in Total Quality activities.

1E INVOLVEMENT WITH CUSTOMERS AND SUPPLIERS

Areas to address could include *how* managers take positive steps to:

- meet, understand and respond to the needs of customers and suppliers
- establish and participate in 'partnership' relationships and joint improvement activities with customers and suppliers.

1F ACTIVE PROMOTION OF TOTAL QUALITY OUTSIDE THE ORGANIZATION

Areas to address could include *how* managers promote Total Quality outside the organization through:

- active participation in professional bodies

- publication of booklets, articles
- presentations at conferences, seminars
- listening, understanding and responding to local community.

Policy and strategy – Criterion 2

Definition

The organization's mission, values, vision and strategic direction and the manner in which it achieves them.

How the organization's policy and strategy reflect the concept of Total Quality and how the principles of Total Quality are used in the formulation, deployment, review and improvement of policy and strategy.

Where mission is defined as the purpose or raison d'être *of the organization. It is not so much 'what is our business or function?' as 'why does our business or function exist?' What purpose justifies the continued existence of the business?*

Where values are defined as the understandings and expectations that describe how the organization's people behave and upon which all business relationships are based (e.g., trust, support, truth).

Where vision is defined as statements that describe the kind of organization it wishes to become (e.g., 'we delight customers by anticipating needs and exceeding expectations', 'the community takes pride in our presence and society values our contribution').

Criterion parts

Self-assessment should demonstrate:

2A HOW POLICY AND STRATEGY ARE FORMULATED ON THE CONCEPT OF TOTAL QUALITY

Areas to address could include *how*:

- Total Quality is reflected in the organization's mission, values, vision and strategy statements
- the organization's policy and strategy are formulated
- the organization balances the needs and expectations of various stakeholders.

2B   HOW POLICY AND STRATEGY ARE BASED ON INFORMATION THAT IS RELEVANT AND COMPREHENSIVE

Areas to address could include *how* use is made of:

- feedback from customers and suppliers
- feedback from the organization's people
- data on performance of competitors and 'best in class' organizations
- data on social, regulatory and legislative issues
- appropriate economic indicators.

2C   HOW POLICY AND STRATEGY ARE THE BASIS FOR BUSINESS PLANS

Areas to address could include *how*:

- policy and strategy are cascaded and implemented through all process levels of the organization
- policy and strategy are a basis for the planning of activities and setting of objectives throughout the organization
- business plans are tested, evaluated, improved, aligned and prioritized within the organization's policy and strategy.

2D   HOW POLICY AND STRATEGY ARE COMMUNICATED INTERNALLY AND EXTERNALLY

Areas to address could include *how*:

- meetings and other personal means of communication are used
- newsletters, posters, videos and other media are used
- communications on policy and strategy are planned and prioritized
- the organization evaluates the awareness of people to its policy and strategy.

2E   HOW POLICY AND STRATEGY ARE REGULARLY UPDATED AND IMPROVED

Areas to address could include *how*:

- the organization evaluates the relevance and effectiveness of its policy and strategy
- the organization reviews and improves its policy and strategy.

People management – Criterion 3

Definition

The management of the organization's people.

How the organization releases the full potential of its people to improve its business continuously.

Where people includes all of the individuals employed by the organization.

Criterion parts

Self-assessment should demonstrate:

3A HOW PEOPLE RESOURCES ARE PLANNED AND IMPROVED

Areas to address could include *how*:

- the human resources strategy plan aligns with the organization's policy and strategy
- surveys of people satisfaction are put into effect and data used
- the organization ensures fairness in terms of employment
- the organization aligns its remuneration, redeployment, redundancy and other terms of employment with its policy and strategy
- the organization encourages the optimum performance and commitment of its people.

3B HOW THE SKILLS AND CAPABILITIES OF THE PEOPLE ARE PRESERVED AND DEVELOPED THROUGH RECRUITMENT, TRAINING AND CAREER PROGRESSION

Areas to address could include *how*:

- people's skills are classified and are matched with the organization's requirements
- recruitment, career development, redeployment and redundancy are managed
- training plans are established and implemented
- the effectiveness of training is reviewed
- people are developed through teamwork.

3C HOW PEOPLE AND TEAMS AGREE TARGETS AND CONTINUOUSLY REVIEW PERFORMANCE

Areas to address could include *how*:

- objectives of individuals and teams are aligned with organizational targets and are agreed upon
- objectives of individuals and teams are reviewed and updated
- people are appraised and helped.

3D HOW THE INVOLVEMENT OF EVERYONE IN CONTINUOUS IMPROVEMENT IS PROMOTED AND PEOPLE ARE EMPOWERED TO TAKE APPROPRIATE ACTION

Areas to address could include *how*:

- people are encouraged to participate constructively in improvement activities
- in-house conferences and ceremonies are used to encourage involvement of people in continuous improvement
- awareness and involvement of people in Health and Safety issues is promoted
- individuals and teams contribute to quality improvement
- people are empowered to take action and how effectiveness is evaluated.

3E HOW EFFECTIVE TOP-DOWN, BOTTOM-UP AND LATERAL COMMUNICATION IS ACHIEVED

Areas to address could include *how*:

- the organization receives information from its people
- the organization transmits information to its people
- the communication needs of the organization are identified
- the effectiveness of communication is evaluated and improved.

Resources – Criterion 4

Definition

The management, utilization and preservation of resources.

How the organization's resources are effectively deployed in support of policy and strategy.

Criterion parts

Self-assessment should demonstrate how business improvements are achieved continuously by the management of:

4A   FINANCIAL RESOURCES

Where financial resources are defined as the short-term funds required for the day-to-day operation of the business, and the capital funding from various sources (shareholder equity, loan capital, retained earnings, government grants, etc.) required for the longer term financing of the business.
   Areas to address could include *how*:

- financial strategies support policy and strategy
- financial strategies and practices are reviewed and improved
- financial parameters such as cashflow, profitability, costs and margins, assets, working capital and shareholder value are managed for improvement
- investment decisions are evaluated
- 'quality cost' concepts are used
- financial risk is managed.

4B   INFORMATION RESOURCES

Where information resources are defined as business and technical data and other information in all its forms and the means of making the information available and accessible.
   Areas to address could include *how*:

- information strategies support policy and strategy
- information systems are managed for improvement
- information validity, integrity, security and scope are assured and improved
- appropriate and relevant information is made more accessible
- people have access to the information they need to do their jobs.

4C   SUPPLIERS, MATERIALS, BUILDINGS AND EQUIPMENT

Where suppliers are defined as any person or organization providing goods or services to the organization. Where materials are defined as physical items in all their forms including stocks of raw materials, finished products and material in progress.
   Areas to address could include *how*:

- management of supplier relationships reflects policy and strategy
- the supply chain is managed for improvements
- material inventories are optimized
- equipment and buildings are managed and utilized to optimum effect
- global non-renewable resources are conserved, recycled and waste minimized
- environmental impact of products, services, sites, etc. are addressed.

4D THE APPLICATION OF TECHNOLOGY

Where application of technology covers how the organization develops and protects technologies, including information technologies, that are the basis of its products, processes and systems and how it explores related and new technologies that may be exploited to the benefit of its business.
Areas to address could include *how*:

- existing technology has been exploited
- alternative and emerging technologies are identified and evaluated according to their impact on the business and their impact on society
- the development of people's skills and capabilities is harmonized with the development of technology
- technology is harnessed in support of improvement in processes and information systems and other systems
- intellectual property is protected and exploited.

Processes – Criterion 5

Definition

The management of all value-adding activities within the organization.

How processes are identified, reviewed and, if necessary, revised to ensure continuous improvement of the organization's business.
Where a process is defined as a sequence of steps which adds value by producing required outputs from a variety of inputs.

Criterion parts

Self-assessment should demonstrate:

5A   HOW PROCESSES CRITICAL TO THE SUCCESS OF THE BUSINESS ARE IDENTIFIED

The response should include a list of your critical processes.
   Areas to address could include *how*:

- critical processes are defined
- the method of identification is conducted
- interface issues are resolved
- 'impact on the business' is evaluated.

Critical processes will normally include those processes associated with the results criteria – Criteria 6–9. They could also include:

- management of suppliers
- provision of raw materials and supplies
- delivery of product or service
- budgeting and planning
- invoicing and collection of debt
- new product and service development
- management of safety, health, environment
- management of regulatory issues
- manufacturing
- engineering
- reception of orders
- design
- marketing and sales

5B   HOW THE ORGANIZATION SYSTEMATICALLY MANAGES ITS PROCESSES

Areas to address could include *how*:

- process ownership and process management are established
- standards of operation are established and monitored
- performance measures are used in process management
- systems standards, e.g., quality systems such as ISO 9000, environmental systems, health and safety systems, are applied in process management.

5C   HOW PROCESSES ARE REVIEWED AND TARGETS SET FOR IMPROVEMENT

Areas to address could include *how*:

- methods of improvement, incremental and breakthrough, are identified and prioritized
- information from employees, customers, suppliers, other stakeholders, competitors and society, and data from benchmarking is used in setting standards of operation and targets for improvement
- current performance measurements and targets for improvement are related to past achievement
- challenging targets to support policy and strategy are identified and agreed upon.

5D   HOW THE ORGANIZATION STIMULATES INNOVATION AND CREATIVITY IN PROCESS
IMPROVEMENT

Areas to address could include *how*:

– the creative talents of employees are brought to bear in incremental and
  breakthrough improvements
– new principles of design, new technology and new operating philosophies
  are discovered and utilized
– organizational structures have been changed to encourage innovation and
  creativity
– continuous learning by everyone in the organization is encouraged.

5E   HOW THE ORGANIZATION IMPLEMENTS PROCESS CHANGES AND EVALUATES THE
BENEFITS

Areas to address could include *how*:

– appropriate methods of implementing change are agreed
– new or changed processes are piloted and implementation controlled
– process changes are communicated
– people are trained prior to implementation
– process changes are reviewed to ensure predicted results are achieved.

Customer satisfaction – Criterion 6

Definition

**What the organization is achieving in relation to the satisfaction of its external
customers.**

*Where the external customer is defined as the immediate customer of the
organization and all other customers in the chain of distribution of its products
and services through to the final customer.*

Criterion parts

Self-assessment should demonstrate the organization's success in satisfying
the needs and expectations of its external customers.

6A   THE CUSTOMERS' PERCEPTION OF THE ORGANIZATION'S PRODUCTS, SERVICES AND
CUSTOMER RELATIONSHIPS

Areas to address could include customers' perceptions (from customer surveys, focus groups and vendor ratings, etc.) with respect to product and service quality of:

- capability of meeting product and service specifications
- reliability of products and services
- delivery performance
- price
- service-level performance
- sales and technical support
- product training
- accessibility of key staff
- documentation
- responsiveness and flexibility in meeting customer needs
- complaints handling
- warranty and guarantee provisions
- development of new products and services.

6B ADDITIONAL MEASURES RELATING TO THE SATISFACTION OF THE ORGANIZA-
TION'S CUSTOMERS

Areas to address could include measurement of:

- repeat business
- new or lost business
- defect, error and rejection rates
- delivery performance
- product or service consistency
- product durability and maintainability
- complaints handling
- letters of praise or thanks received
- corrective actions resulting from complaints
- warranty payments
- guarantee provisions made and used
- awards and accolades received
- publicity levels in the media.

People satisfaction – Criterion 7

Definition

What the organization is achieving in relation to the satisfaction of its people.

Where people are defined as all of the individuals employed by the organization.

Criterion parts

Self-assessment should demonstrate the organization's success in satisfying the needs and expectations of its people.

7A   THE PEOPLE'S PERCEPTION OF THE ORGANIZATION

Areas to address could include people's perceptions (from employee surveys, focus groups, suggestions schemes, annual reviews, etc.) of:

Factors relating to motivation:
- opportunity to achieve
- empowerment
- involvement
- career development
- training and retraining
- recognition
- appraisal and target setting
- improvement process.

Factors relating to satisfaction:
- the organization's mission, values, vision and strategy
- employment conditions
- reward schemes
- working environment
- health and safety provisions
- job security
- relationships with: supervisor, peers, others
- communication
- company administration
- the organization's role in the community and society
- the organization's environmental impact and policy.

7B   ADDITIONAL MEASURES RELATING TO PEOPLE SATISFACTION

Areas to address could include measurement of:

Factors relating to satisfaction:
- levels of training and development
- recognition of individuals and teams
- absenteeism and sickness
- grievances
- staff turnover
- accident levels

- recruitment trends
- the use of organization-provided facilities (e.g., recreational, medical, creche).

Factors relating to people involvement:
- participation in improvement teams
- involvement in suggestion schemes
- measurable benefits of teamwork.

Impact on society – Criterion 8

Definition

What the organization is achieving in satisfying the needs and the expectations of the community at large. This includes perception of the organization's approach to quality of life, to the environment and to the preservation of global resources, and the organization's own internal measures.

Criterion parts

Self-assessment should demonstrate the organization's success in satisfying the needs and expectations of the community at large.

8A   THE PERCEPTION OF THE COMMUNITY AT LARGE OF THE ORGANIZATION'S IMPACT ON SOCIETY

Areas to address could include (from surveys, reports, media, public meetings, etc.) the *community's* perception of the organization's:

- impact on local employment levels and the local economy
- active involvement in the community, including:
  - support for charity
  - involvement in education and training
  - support for sport and leisure
  - support for medical and welfare provision
- activities to assist the preservation of global resources, including:
  - energy conservation
  - usage of recycled materials
  - reduction of waste
  - use of raw materials or other inputs
  - environmental and ecological impact
- activities to reduce and prevent nuisance and harm to neighbours as a result of its operations, including:

- pollution levels
- hazards
- noise
- health risks.

8B   ADDITIONAL MEASURES RELATING TO THE ORGANIZATION'S IMPACT ON SOCIETY

Areas to address could include measurements of the organization's:

- impact on local employment levels and the local economy
- active involvement in the community, including:
  - support for charity
  - involvement in education and training
  - support for sport and leisure
  - support for medical and welfare provision
- activities to assist the preservation of global resources, including:
  - energy conservation
  - usage of recycled materials
  - reduction of waste
  - use of raw materials or other inputs
  - environmental and ecological impact
- activities to reduce and prevent nuisance and harm to neighbours as a result of its operations, including:
  - pollution levels
  - hazards
  - noise
  - health risks.

Other indicators could include:

- accolades and awards received
- number of infringements of national and international standards and regulations
- complaint levels
- number of safety-related incidents
- reports from external inspectors and regulators.

Business results – Criterion 9

Definition

What the organization is achieving in relation to its planned business performance and in satisfying the needs and expectations of everyone with a

financial interest in the organization, and in achieving its planned business objectives.

Criterion parts

Self-assessment should demonstrate:

9A   FINANCIAL MEASURES OF THE ORGANIZATION'S SUCCESS

Areas to address could include:

- profit and loss account items such as sales, gross margins, net profit
- balance sheet items such as total assets, working capital (including inventory turnover), long-term borrowings and shareholders' funds
- cashflow items, such as operating cashflow, capital expenditure and financing cashflows
- other relevant indicators such as value added, return on net assets and return on equity
- credit ratings
- long-term shareholder value (total shareholder returns).

(Several of the above can be expressed in absolute terms or as ratios per unit of capital or per person employed.)

9B   NON-FINANCIAL MEASURES OF THE ORGANIZATION'S SUCCESS

These will include internal efficiency and effectiveness measures vital to the organization's continuing success. Many of the measures will be related to the critical processes listed in Criterion part 5A.
    Areas to address could include:

- market share
- supplier performance
- variability and process capability
- defects per unit of output or activity
- waste and non-value adding activities
- cycle times, such as:
    - order processing time
    - product and delivery time
    - time to resolve complaints
    - batch processing time
    - time to bring new products and services to market
    - inventory turnover time.

Index

Other titles of interest from the McGraw-Hill Quality in Action Series

Quality of Service – Making it Really Work
Bo Edvardsson, Bertil Thomasson and John Øvretveit
0 07 707949-3

Japanese-Led Companies – Understanding How to Make Them Your Customers
Nigel Holden and Matt Burgess
0 07 707817-9

Communicating Change
Bill Quirke
0 07 707941-8

Motivating Your Organization – Achieving Business Success through Reward and Recognition
Colin Pitts
0 07 707967-1

Other recent management titles by McGraw-Hill

Succeeding with Change – Implementing Action-driven Strategies
Tony Eccles
0 07 709004-7

Building the Responsive Organization – Using Employee Surveys to Manage Change
Mike Walters
0 07 709021-7

Forthcoming

Vision at Work – Decision-Making Strategy for the Business Leader
John Mitchell
0 07 709085-3

Leadership for Quality – Strategies for Action
Frances Clark
0 07 707828-4